DILAPIDATIONS

Jason Hunter

Acknowledgements

Crown copyright material is reproduced with the permission of the controller of HMSO and the Queen's Printer for Scotland.

Please note: References to the masculine include, where appropriate, the feminine.

Published by RICS Business Services Limited

a wholly owned subsidiary of

The Royal Institution of Chartered Surveyors

under the RICS Books imprint

Surveyor Court

Westwood Business Park

Coventry CV4 8JE

UK

www.ricsbooks.com

ISBN 1 84219 240 X

Typeset in Great Britain by Columns Design Ltd, Reading, Berks

Printed in Great Britain by Great Britain by Bell & Bain, Glasgow

Contents

Contents

Contents

Preface

While chartered surveyors may not need the *breadth* of understanding of the law of their opposite numbers in the legal profession, in a number of key areas of application to property and construction they need a similar *depth* of knowledge. Exactly what the key areas may be depends to some extent on the nature of the surveyor's practice. Two obvious examples are the law of landlord and tenant, and town and country planning. There are plenty of surveyors who know more than the average lawyer in general practice about the *law* relating to rent reviews or compulsory purchase obligations, as well, obviously, as procedural and valuation aspects.

So surveyors need law and, for a variety of reasons, need to maintain and develop their understanding of it. Changing trends or individual variations in clients' requirements mean that from time to time even the best practitioners (perhaps especially the best practitioners) will feel the need to expand their legal knowledge. The knowledge acquired at college, or in studying for the RICS Assessment of Profession Competence (APC), has a limited shelf life and needs to be constantly updated to maintain its currency. Even specialists working in their areas of expertise need a source of reference as an aide-mémoire or as a first port of call in more detailed research.

The Case in Point series

RICS Books is committed to meeting the needs of surveying (and other) professionals and the Case in Point series typifies that commitment. It is aimed at those who need to upgrade or update their legal knowledge or who need to have access to a good first reference at the outset of an inquiry. A particular difficulty is the burgeoning of reported decisions of the courts. The sheer scale of the law reports, both general and specialist, makes it very hard even to be aware of recent trends, let alone identify the significance of a particular decision. Thus it was decided to focus on developments in case law. In any given matter, the practitioner will want to be directed efficiently and painlessly to the decision that bears upon the matter he or she is dealing with, in other words to 'the case in point'.

The books in the Case in Point series offer a wealth of legal information which is essential in its practical application to the surveyor's work. The authors have the level of expertise required to be selective and succinct, thus achieving a high degree of relevance without sacrificing accessibility. The series has developed incrementally and now forms a collection of specialist handbooks which can deliver what practitioners need – the law on the matter they are handling, when they want it.

Dilapidations, Jason Hunter

The word 'dilapidations' is something of an anachronism, although everyone in the property industry knows its general meaning. No better, or at least no widely accepted, term has been found to describe issues of condition, maintenance, damage and repair of real estate.

It is an inescapable fact that properties deteriorate. The law of dilapidations determines the allocation of responsibilities and the resultant financial burden. It thus forms part of the landlord and tenant battleground. The stakes can be high. The extent of the Schedule of Dilapidations on the termination of a tenancy will in some cases actually constitute the difference between the success or failure of an investment. Not surprisingly, it has therefore given rise to a very large volume of litigation. The area has been the subject of recent and generally welcomed guidance, most notably the Property Litigation Association's *Protocol for Terminal Dilapidations Claims for Damages* and the RICS guidance note, *Dilapidations*.

But, as so often with property law, answers to questions on the law of dilapidations are not to be found in a convenient statute or any other easily accessible source, although legislation (in the form of successive *Rent Acts* and *Housing Acts* and notably the *Leasehold Property (Repairs) Act* 1938 and the *Landlord and Tenant (Covenants) Act* 1995) has had a significant influence.

To get an accurate and detailed view of the law of dilapidations and answers to questions on it, an appraisal of the case law is inevitable. This necessitates going back over a century to cases like *Walker v Hatton* (1842) and *Proudfoot v Hart* (1890), the latter still a leading authority on the interpretation of standard of repair. It also necessitates coming forward to recent major decisions like *Mason v Totalfinaelf UK Ltd* (2003) on that issue and *Simmons v Dresden* (2004) on dilapidations claims. The task of identifying and analysing the key decisions which form the modern law on dilapidations from a body of cases spanning two centuries is not one for the gifted amateur.

Jason Hunter has already written extensively for RICS, the Law Society and professional journals on property law in general and dilapidations in particular. But even more important, he brings to bear on the subject very substantial professional experience as a property litigation solicitor, as Head of the Contentious Property Department with London firm Russell-Cooke.

Successively Vice-Chairman and Chairman of the Property Litigation Association, Jason headed the Association's Law Reform Committee and was closely involved with the production of the Dilapidations Protocol and the government's consultation exercise on the reform of the *Landlord and Tenant Act* 1954. The end product therefore exhibits practical relevance as well as mastery of the case law.

Anthony Lavers, 2005.
Professional Support Lawyer, White and Case, London.
Visiting Professor of Law, Oxford Brookes University.
Consultant Editor, Case in Point series.

Introduction

Properties are designed to work and function in a particular way. If property is not looked after, it can fall into disrepair and damage can be caused to it or to the people using it. Property that is out of repair or has not been well maintained is of less use to those who own or occupy it. In such circumstances, it is of less intrinsic value.

Therefore, where a property (or part of it) is let, the owner (the landlord) and occupier (the tenant) will want to make sure that someone is responsible for looking after it. In the case of the tenant, it will want to ensure that the property is fit for the purposes it wants to use it. In the case of the landlord, it will want to ensure that the property's physical integrity and, therefore, value is preserved not only during the course of the tenancy but so that it can be re-let at the end of the tenancy.

In almost all written tenancies, there will be obligations concerning the form and condition of the property; some tenancies (written or not) are silent on the subject, yet some such obligations are implied whether by case law or statute.

These obligations seek to dictate, among other things, the manner in which, or the extent to which, the property that is the subject of the tenancy is put or kept in repair, decorated, altered, used and the condition it should be in at the end of the tenancy.

A failure to comply with such obligations can give rise to a claim for what is commonly known as 'dilapidations'.

While there are a number of relevant statutory provisions, the law concerning dilapidations has evolved largely through decisions of the courts. From such decisions, one can (sometimes) discern principles that influence the manner in which property is maintained or used.

However, one frequently hears lawyers say that a case 'turns on its own facts'. In other words, while there may be issues of general application which may assist in one's attempts to resolve a particular problem, ultimately one cannot say with absolute certainty what the answer or outcome might be. This is particularly true of dilapidations. There are very few identical properties and very few identical leases. The fact that properties and tenancy terms differ inevitably means that, if there is a dispute, it can only be resolved on the basis of an understanding and interpretation of the problems and issues specific to the property and lease concerned. Hence the uncertainty of outcome. All that said, as will be observed, there have been some cases to which one can make frequent reference as a result of their applicability to a range of dilapidations principles (such as *Gibson Investments Ltd v Chesterton plc* (No. 1) (2002)).

One of the ways by which this difficulty can be eased is by the facilitation of uniformity of basic practice. It is impossible to prescribe practice for all cases because, as described in the preceding paragraph, dilapidations cases will not be identical. However, publications like the Royal Institution of Chartered Surveyors' guidance note on *Dilapidations* (the Guidance Note) or the Property Litigation Association's *Protocol for Terminal Dilapidations Claims for Damages* (the Protocol) go some way to ensuring that, at the very least, there should be some similarity of approach when considering how to deal with a dilapidations problem.

This book is intended to act as an accessible guide to the practice of dilapidations, illustrating particular problems by reference to relevant cases. It is intended to supplement the practical advice contained in the Guidance Note and the Protocol but not to supersede it. It is not meant to be a substitute for the excellent, intricate, more 'legal' analysis of the law of dilapidations in such learned works as *Dilapidations – The Modern Law and Practice* by Nicholas Dowding QC and Kirk Reynolds QC or *The Handbook of Dilapidations* by Del Williams. Nor is it meant to be a substitute for specialist legal advice on specific problems. The majority of dilapidations claims are resolved between the landlord and tenant, often with the assistance of a surveyor and without the need either for such legal advice or for legal proceedings. This book is intended to assist the reader in better understanding the law of dilapidations and, it is to be hoped, to aid in the resolution of dilapidations problems.

With that in mind, this book is structured in a manner that aims to follow, as much as possible, the approach that a surveyor would adopt when considering a dilapidations problem.

Being part of the Case in Point series of publications, it seeks to do so, wherever possible, by using cases to illustrate dilapidations issues. However, there will not always be a case to illustrate every point that is made.

Almost the first thing I was taught when I started my training to be a solicitor was, when faced with a landlord and tenant problem, 'Always look at the lease!'. That is particularly true of dilapidations claims. Thus, the early chapters consider the tenancy and its terms and how they are to be identified (not all of them will be in the lease itself).

The text then considers particular types of obligation, any limitations on them, whether they have been broken and, if so, what needs to be done to put it right. There is a consideration of the remedies open to the landlord or tenant if the broken obligations are not remedied and any limitations on those options. As the text progresses, it will pick up on common problems.

Since the resolution of dilapidations claims is frequently a practical exercise conducted by practical people, there will not necessarily be cases that illustrate every aspect of a dilapidations claim, simply because some points never become the subject of reported decisions of the courts. Indeed, following the implementation of the *Civil Procedure Rules* in April 1999, those involved in disputes (whether concerning dilapidations or not) are encouraged to make a greater effort to resolve them without involving the courts. That 'encouragement' takes the form of sanctions if a court finds that a party to a dispute it has been required to consider has behaved unreasonably before or during the litigation. Those sanctions can be the award of higher costs, the deduction of costs, the award of higher interest on monetary claims and so on. Therefore, armed with the Guidance Note, the Protocol and texts such as this, one hopes that even fewer cases result in active litigation.

Many of the legal issues and cases discussed in the text concern commercial property. However, more often than not, the principles are of equal application to residential property. Indeed, some of the leading 'dilapidations' cases concern residential property. In the particular case of residential property, there are specific issues arising from statutory provisions and these will be considered separately (in the main and in the context of dilapidations claims, they concern terms implied into a residential tenancy). Further, many of the issues are discussed in the context of tenants' obligations; however, the principles almost always apply to landlord's obligations too. Where there are issues of specific relevance to claims by tenants against landlords, they will be considered separately (primarily, they relate to issues of enforcement).

Finally, some brief acknowledgements. Some of the material in this book is based on material published by RICS Books in the *Dilapidations* chapter of the online service *isurv dispute resolution*, which Mark Tatlow, Patricia Vassallo and I co-authored. I must also thank Edward Shaw and Peter Beckett, both well-known surveyors involved in different aspects of dilapidations work and active members of the RICS Dilapidations panel; they both were kind enough to review the text and make extremely helpful suggestions.

List of Acts, Statutory Instruments and abbreviations

The following Acts and Statutory Instruments are referred to in this publication.

Where an Act or Statutory Instrument is mentioned frequently, it is referred to by the abbreviation in brackets that follows.

Criminal Law Act 1977

Defective Premises Act 1972

Disability Discrimination Act 1995 (**'the DDA'**)

Health and Safety at Work etc. Act 1974

Housing Act 1961

Housing Act 1988

Land Registration Act 2002

Landlord and Tenant (Covenants) Act 1995 (**'the 1995 Act'**)

Landlord and Tenant Act 1927 (**'the 1927 Act'**)

Landlord and Tenant Act 1954

Landlord and Tenant Act 1985

Landlord and Tenant Act 1987

Law of Property Act 1925 (**'the 1925 Act'**)

Leasehold Property (Repairs) Act 1938 (**'the 1938 Act'**)

Limitation Act 1980

Metropolitan Building Act 1855

Occupiers Liability Act 1957

Occupiers Liability Act 1984

Protection from Eviction Act 1977

Rent Act 1977

Statute of Frauds 1677

Civil Procedure Rules 1998 (SI 1998/3132)

Construction (Design and Management) Regulations 1994 (SI 1994/3140)

Control of Asbestos at Work Regulations 2002 (SI 2002/2675)

The text of this publication is divided into commentary and case summaries. The commentary is enclosed between grey highlighted lines for ease of reference.

Table of cases

1
The tenancy

1.1 INTRODUCTION

To be able to understand the legal relationship between the landlord and the tenant, one has to identify the terms of the tenancy and to what it relates.

If the tenancy is in writing, then that written document will be the first port of call. The terms that are set out in writing are described as 'express terms'. However, despite the length of modern leases (the document which records the agreement creating the tenancy), it is often the case that some issue or other is left unaddressed.

In some cases (and particularly in the case of residential property), the law will either leave unfilled any gap (lacuna) in the tenancy arrangements or it will imply a term by, as it were, legal reasoning or an of Parliament. A typical example of the latter would be the repairing obligation implied into short residential leases by section 11 of the *Landlord and Tenant Act 1985* (see 1.6 below). These obligations are known as 'implied terms'.

Collectively, the express and any implied terms should define the relationship between the landlord and tenant. Thus, one should be able to identify the property demised by the tenancy, the period of the tenancy, the obligations of the landlord and the tenant (including in relation to the form and condition of the property), the amount of rent to be paid, the obligations of others (e.g. a guarantor) and other matters that have been agreed (e.g. that the tenancy may be brought to an end in certain circumstances).

1.2 THE EXPRESS TERMS OF THE TENANCY

To identify and understand the express terms of the tenancy that relate to the form and condition of the property demised by the tenancy, one must identify and consider the documents relating to the tenancy. These may include:

1

- the lease;
- any deeds of variation;
- any licences for alterations;
- any other licences or deeds that relate to the state and condition of the property;
- if the lease is an underlease, any superior lease;
- any schedules of condition or surveys;
- any plans or drawings of the property;
- any photographs showing the property in a fully maintained condition;
- any subtenancies;
- any letters (i.e. side letters) concerning the state and condition of the property.

The frequently encountered obligations (known as covenants) will be considered in greater depth below.

But to put the covenants into context, the first thing to do is to understand the extent of the property demised by the lease (see 1.7).

1.3 THE IMPLIED TERMS OF THE TENANCY

Where the terms of a tenancy are not in writing or the written tenancy leaves issues unaddressed, the law sometimes implies terms into the tenancy to make it 'work' effectively. Sometimes, notwithstanding the written terms of the tenancy, the law implies different terms whether by statute or not, e.g. the repairing obligation implied into short residential leases by section 11 of the *Landlord and Tenant Act* 1985 (see 1.6 below).

In practice, there are three situations in which terms will be implied into a tenancy:

- those implied by what is known as common law (i.e. not by statute) being

  (i) those incorporated into a specific tenancy for specific reasons;

  (ii) those always capable of being incorporated into all tenancies in certain circumstances;

and

- (iii) those incorporated by statute.

1.3.1 Terms implied by common law

1.3.1.1 Terms implied in specific cases

While modern leases are often extremely lengthy, there are still occasions when a situation arises which will not have been catered for. When one analyses the express tenancy terms, one might find that either nothing has been said at all about the problem concerned or there is a gap in the terms leaving the landlord and tenant unclear as to which of them has responsibility for the problem. But just because there is a gap in the terms of the tenancy, the court will not always seek to resolve it. The more obviously detailed and complete the lease, the less likely it is that the court will intervene to plug a gap.

Duke of Westminster v Guild (1985)

In the case of a lease that made 'careful and elaborate' provision for the repair and maintenance of property, the court concluded that, if it had been intended that other contractual repairing obligations should be placed on the landlord, the lease would have made provision for them. Therefore, the term the tenant asked the court to imply was rejected.

Jacey Property Co Ltd v Miguel De Sousa and another (2003)

In a case concerning a lease which did not provide for the repair of drains, the court would not re-write the lease to fill the gap left by the draftsman.

BP Refinery (Westernport) Pty Ltd v Shire of Hastings (1978)

The court established a five-point test when considering whether or not to imply a term into a contract (which includes a lease):

1   The term must be reasonable and equitable.

2   The term must be necessary to give business efficacy to the lease.

3

3 The term must be an obvious one to imply into the lease.

4 The term must be capable of being clearly expressed.

5 The term must not contradict any express term of the lease.

The more comprehensive the scheme for repairs expressly provided for in the lease, the less likely it is that a term will be implied.

Holding & Barnes plc v Hill House Hammond Ltd (2001)

Where there appeared to be a gap in the obligations to repair the structure and exterior of the property, the Court of Appeal determined that, on the facts of the case and in the context of the specific lease concerned, there was an implied obligation on the landlord to repair the structure and exterior. The court was satisfied that that was what the landlord and tenant had in fact intended.

Petersson v Pitt Place (Epsom) Ltd (2001)

In a case where there appeared to be overlapping repairing obligations, the court concluded that such a consequence was so impractical that it had to be avoided unless, on the specific language used in the lease, it could not be. As a consequence, where both the landlord and the tenants could have been responsible for the repair of roof terraces, the Court of Appeal held that the tenants were.

Ibrahim v Dovecorn Reversions Ltd (2001)

By contrast with *Petersson*, in the case of the lease considered in *Ibrahim*, the judge concluded that the roof terrace was within the definition of 'main structure' and therefore the responsibility of the landlord.

1.3.1.2 Terms capable of being implied in all cases in certain circumstances

Some covenants are implied into any tenancy. For example, there is always an implied covenant that the landlord will allow the tenant to quietly enjoy the property demised to it if there is no such express covenant. There could only be an express covenant for quiet enjoyment if the tenancy is in writing, but not every lease contains one.

1.4 IMPLIED LANDLORD COVENANTS

1.4.1 To repair the property or part of it

With some exceptions, if the tenancy is silent about repairs or if it imposes some repairing obligations but does not impose them on the landlord, generally the court will not impose an obligation on the landlord to carry out repairs. That is even more likely to be the case if the lease is otherwise comprehensive.

Duke of Westminster v Guild (1985)

In a case where the lease did not include a covenant on the part of the landlord to repair certain parts of the property, there were no special factors requiring the lease to be construed to give it business efficacy by imposing on the lessors the onerous obligation to carry out works of repair. Therefore, the general rule that there was no implied covenant that a lessor was under an obligation to carry out works of repair applied.

Demetriou v Poolaction Ltd and another (1991)

In a case of the renewal of a business tenancy under the *Landlord and Tenant Act* 1954 in which the question as to whether or not the landlord was under a repairing obligation was relevant, the Court of Appeal said:

'Moreover, it is a phenomenon, certainly known at common law, that there may be situations in which there is no repairing obligation imposed either expressly or impliedly on anyone in relation to a lease.'

But there are circumstances in which the general rule will be disapplied and a covenant implied against the landlord. It would seem that the court could imply a repairing obligation where:

- the landlord retains control of the means of access or facilities essential to the enjoyment of the property and

- where the tenant is under an express obligation to do something and that can only be effective if the landlord is under a correlative obligation.

1.4.2 Means of access

Liverpool City Council v Irwin (1977)

Liverpool City Council owned a tower block containing some 70 dwelling units. Over the years the condition of the block deteriorated. The defects included the continual failure of lifts, lack of proper stair lighting and blockage of the rubbish chutes. In addition, the badly designed lavatory cisterns had overflowed causing damage to the property. Mr and Mrs Irwin together with other tenants protested against the condition of the block by refusing to pay rent to the corporation. The corporation sought an order for possession of the property and Mr and Mrs Irwin counterclaimed against them alleging a breach on the part of the corporation of its implied covenant for their quiet enjoyment of the property. While the trial judge granted an order for possession, it was contended that there was an implied obligation on the corporation to keep the staircase and corridors of the block in repair and the lights in working order, and that the corporation was in breach of the obligation. It had not, however, been shown that the corporation had failed to take reasonable care.

The defect in the design of the cisterns constituted a breach by the corporation of the covenant implied by section 32(1)(b)(i) of the *Housing Act* 1961. Accordingly the appellants were entitled to nominal damages of £5 for breach of that covenant and the appeal was allowed to that extent.

King v South Northamptonshire DC (1992)

The issue was whether or not the landlord had responsibility for a footpath leading to the property. One of the Court of Appeal judges said:

'I approach the problem from the basis that the expressed terms of the tenancy, as derived from the conditions of tenancy, were incomplete. They were incomplete because they lacked any obligation upon the landlord at all.

In order to give the arrangement a necessary bilateral character, the landlord's obligations have to be derived by implication of law ... As a matter of general law, it is not to be implied that there is an obligation upon a landlord to maintain retained land over which a right has been granted to the tenant.'

In the circumstances of the case, he concluded that the landlord was nonetheless under an obligation to repair the path.

1.4.3 Correlative obligation

It would seem that the circumstances in which a court will imply a correlative obligation fall into two categories:

- where the tenant has to pay for the cost of some work carried out by the landlord, in which case the landlord may be obliged to carry out the work; and
- where the tenant has to do some work but cannot do so without the landlord having a repairing obligation too.

Barnes v City of London Real Property Co (1918)

The landlords had let various sets of rooms and by the tenancy agreement had imposed on the tenants the obligation to pay a stated additional rent specifically for the cleaning of rooms by a housekeeper to be provided for the purpose. The agreements placed no express obligation on the landlords to provide for the cleaning of the rooms, but the court was of the clear opinion that such an obligation should be implied.

The case has been distinguished in later cases (e.g. *Duke of Westminster v Guild*) because it was a much stronger case than the later cases concerned, if only because the obligation of the tenants to pay the rent for the particular service was an unqualified obligation to pay a definite periodic amount in respect of that service, the obligation to pay not being expressed so as to be conditional on the provision of the service or on the service of notice requesting payment.

Russell v Laimond Properties Ltd (1984)

In a case where the tenant was not obliged to pay for porterage services unless they were provided, then it would seem that an obligation to provide such services (or carry out work) would not generally be imposed upon the landlord.

Barrett v Lounova (1982) Ltd (1990)

An obligation on the landlord to repair the outside of property could be implied into a tenancy agreement where it was necessary to do so to give business efficacy to the agreement. Accordingly, where a tenancy agreement contained an express covenant by the tenant to keep the inside of the property in repair but was silent as to any obligation to repair the outside, and the tenant's covenant was intended to be enforceable throughout the tenancy and could not be properly performed unless the outside was kept in repair, an obligation by the landlord to repair the outside, correlative to the tenant's obligation to repair the inside, could be implied in order to give business efficacy to the agreement. In the circumstances of the case, such a term would be implied.

1.4.4 To repair property retained by the landlord

Cockburn v Smith (1924)

The landlord retained the roof and gutters of a property in which a flat was let to the tenant. Although there were no express repairing obligations on the landlord in respect of the roof and guttering, when damp affected the flat as a result of defects in them, the landlord was held responsible.

Gordon v Selico Co Ltd (1986)

However, where there is comprehensive provision for repairs in a written tenancy agreement, it will generally mean that there are no grounds for implying such a term in relation to retained (or common) parts.

1.4.5 Furnished houses, builder-landlords and property being constructed

Covenants can also be imposed upon the landlord in the case of furnished houses (that they should be fit for habitation), where the landlord is also the builder of the property (the property should not be defectively built) and where the property is in the course of construction (on completion, it should be fit for the contemplated use).

1.5 IMPLIED TENANT COVENANTS

In the case of most modern lettings of commercial property, it is quite rare to find that they contain no tenants' repairing obligations. The same is true for most residential lettings (whether short or long). However, perhaps particularly in the case of residential property, there are occasions when a tenancy is entered into informally or, as it were, by accident. In such cases, the terms of the tenancy will be those implied.

In relation to the form and condition of the property, there are four categories of covenant implied in respect of tenants. Since most tenancies carry more onerous, express obligations, they will only be touched on briefly.

1.5.1 The tenant must use the property in a tenant-like manner

The nature of the covenant was explained in *Warren v Keen* (see below). It would seem to cover a large number of relatively minor things. But it will not always operate either because the nature of the tenant's 'behaviour' does not fall within the covenant or because there is an express covenant the nature of which leads one to conclude that the express covenant was intended to preclude other, implied, covenants such as that of tenant-like user from operating.

Warren v Keen (1954)

'The tenant must take proper care of the property. He must, if he is going away for the winter, turn off the water and empty the boiler; he must clean the chimneys, when necessary, and also the windows; he must mend the electric light when it fuses ... he must do the little jobs about the place which a reasonable tenant would do. In addition, he must not, of course, damage the house wilfully or negligently; and he must see that his family and guests do not damage it – if they do, he must repair it. But, apart from such things, if the house falls into disrepair

9

through fair wear and tear or lapse of time or for any reason not caused by him, the tenant is not liable to repair it.'

Wycombe Area Health Authority v Barnett (1982)

In this case, where the water supply passed through a pipe which was not lagged and which burst during cold weather while the tenant was away for a slightly longer period than anticipated, the tenant was not in breach of the implied covenant of tenant-like user for failing to either empty the water system or to lag the pipe.

1.5.2 The property must be kept water and windtight

Dowding and Reynolds note (at section 21–08) that there is case law which suggests the existence of an implied covenant that the tenant should keep the demised property water- and windtight. However, they conclude that if there was such an obligation, it did not exceed (by way of obligation) the covenant of tenant-like user. In essence, if there was such a covenant, the obligations it created were already within the obligations imposed by the covenant of tenant-like user.

1.5.3 The tenant must not commit 'voluntary waste'

If a tenant deliberately or negligently damages the demised property and in doing so causes harm to the reversionary interest of the landlord, the tenant will have committed voluntary waste. Voluntary waste can also arise where the land is altered thereby changing its character. But using the property in the ordinary way for which it has been let will not be waste.

Mancetter Developments Ltd v Garmanson and Givertz (1986)

The common law duty to make good or repair damage to property caused by the removal of tenant's or trade fixtures included in this case an obligation to fill in holes left in the walls of a property when the fixtures were removed if the holes affected the structure rather than just the decoration of the property. While the fixtures remained installed the property remained weatherproof but without the fixtures the property was no longer weatherproof and the reversion was adversely affected. For that reason also, the burden of filling in the holes lay on the person who removed the fixtures, because that was when the waste occurred, and not on the person who made the holes. Waste was committed when there was a failure to fill up the holes left after removing the fans and pipes, because the property then ceased to be weatherproof and was damaged as a result. The filling of screw holes or nail holes where a fixture is removed which has been screwed or nailed to a wall may be a matter de minimis.

West Ham Central Charity Board v East London Waterworks Co (1900)

In a case concerning land which had been let for the purposes of creating a reservoir and which instead was used for dumping rubbish, causing the height of the land to increase such that the landlord could not then do what it wanted with the land without digging it out, the court held that the effect of the alteration by the tenant was that there had been waste. The judge also noted that:

'If the permanent character of the property demised is not substantially altered, as for instance, by the conversion of pasture land into plough land, by breaking up ancient meadows, or the like, I conceive that the law is that it is not now waste for the tenant to do things which within the covenants and conditions of his lease he is not precluded from doing. Within those covenants and conditions he may use his holding as he pleases.'

1.5.4 The tenant must not commit 'permissive waste'

Whereas voluntary waste involves doing something that causes damage to the property and harms the landlord's reversion or alters the character of the property, permissive waste comes about when, for example, the tenant fails to do something it ought to have done (e.g. carry out repairs). But that does not mean that the covenant not to commit permissive waste is equivalent to a tenant's covenant to repair. However, with time, almost all types of tenancy have been held to be not subject to the implied covenant. As noted by Dowding and Reynolds

11

(sections 21–17 and 21–18), in fact it is probably only fixed-term tenants who are subject to the implied covenant, but even then possibly not if there are express covenants to the contrary.

1.6   TERMS IMPLIED BY STATUTE

Unlike terms implied into tenancies by common law where some directly affect the landlord and some directly affect the tenant, with one exception, those implied by statute primarily concern landlords alone (although, obviously, for the benefit of tenants). The most often encountered (*Landlord and Tenant Act* 1985, section 11) is only concerned with residential property.

Landlord and Tenant Act 1985, section 11

Concerning residential short-term tenancies (under seven years) and entered into on or after 24 October 1961, with some exceptions, section 11 of the *Landlord and Tenant Act* 1985 imposes on landlords an obligation to keep in repair the structure and exterior of the property, to keep in repair and proper working order the installations for the supply of water, gas and electricity and for sanitation (with certain items excluded) and to keep in repair and proper working order the installations for space heating and for heating water. Unlike some landlords' repairing covenants (discussed in Chapter 2), the covenant implied by section 11 only operates when the landlord has notice of the problem or defect before liability arises. Section 11 also implies an obligation on the tenant to give access to inspect the property and section 12 creates a rarely used power in favour of the County Court to exclude section 11 from the tenancy. The terms implied by section 11 were slightly modified and extended by the *Housing Act* 1988 which generally applies to tenancies created on or after 15 January 1989.

Niazi Services Ltd v Van der Loo (2004)

But the liability of the landlord will only arise if the defect complained of is within part of the property belonging to the landlord. The landlord in this case was the long leaseholder of a top-floor flat in Chelsea. The tenant was the subtenant, who had held the property under a series of annual tenancies.

Following a long-running dispute between them over items of disrepair, the tenant withheld his rent. When sued for arrears, he counterclaimed for damages in respect of the landlord's breach of its repairing obligations under section 11. The question was whether the landlord could be held liable in respect of the inadequate water pressure in the flat, which, over a period of almost three years, had reduced the supply to a mere trickle during certain hours of the day. This had been caused by works to the restaurant premises that were located on the ground floor and in the basement of the building. A larger take-off water pipe had been installed as part of the works to the restaurant, which had resulted in the supply problems to the upper floors whenever water was being drawn off in the restaurant. The installation for the supply of water to the tenant's flat was not in proper working order and if he had been the direct tenant of the owner of the building, he would have had a claim under the amended section 11. However, he held a subtenancy from a landlord whose own tenancy related only to the flat itself. His landlord clearly did not own or control the water pipes in the remainder of the building. Therefore, the issue was whether the water pipe formed 'part of any part of a building' in which the landlord had 'an estate or interest'. The court was satisfied that the above limb of the statutory definition required the landlord, not simply to have an estate or interest in any part of the property (which the landlord did — it held a tenancy of the top-floor flat), but to have an estate or interest in that part of the property of which the defective installation formed part (which Niazi did not). This meant that the landlord could not be held legally liable for the poor water supply to the flat.

Rent Act 1977, sections 3 and 148, Housing Act 1988, section 16

Under section 148 of the *Rent Act* 1977 and section 16 of the *Housing Act* 1988 (which both apply to residential lettings that are within the protection of those Acts), there is implied into tenancies regulated, respectively, by the *Rent Act* and the *Housing Act* a term that the tenant shall allow the landlord access to the property to carry out repairs for which the landlord has an obligation to undertake. That will include both express obligations and those implied into the tenancy, for example, by section 11 of the *Landlord and Tenant Act* 1985.

Defective Premises Act 1972, section 4

Where property is let under a tenancy under which the landlord has the repairing obligation (express or implied), by virtue of *Defective Premises Act* 1972, section 4, the landlord is under a duty to all persons (including the tenant) who might reasonably be expected to be affected by defects in the property (defined by section 4(3) as a failure by him to carry out his obligation to the tenant for the maintenance or repair of the property) to take such care as is reasonable in all the circumstances to see that such persons are reasonably safe from personal injury or damage to property. Section 4 can also apply where the landlord has, expressly or impliedly, the right to enter the property to carry out any description of maintenance or repair of the property, so that, as from the time when he first is, or by notice or otherwise can put himself, in a position to exercise the right and so long as he is or can put himself in that position, it is treated for the purposes of the duties under section 4 (but for no other purpose) as if it were under an obligation to the tenant for that description of maintenance or repair of the property. However, the landlord shall not owe the tenant any duty in respect of any defect in the state of the property arising from, or continuing because of, a failure to carry out an obligation expressly imposed on the tenant by the tenancy. Unlike section 11 of the *Landlord and Tenant Act* 1985, there is no scope for contracting out of the duty imposed by section 4.

Occupiers Liability Act 1957

The *Occupiers Liability Act* 1957 imposes on occupiers of property – landlords (where there are premises over which it retains control, e.g. common parts) and tenants – a duty of care to visitors to the property (which can include tenants passing over common parts) that they will be reasonably safe in using the property for the purposes for which they are invited or permitted by the occupier to be there. One should also note the extension of the duties of an occupier effected by the *Occupiers Liability Act* 1984.

Landlord and Tenant Act 1985, section 8

Under section 8 of the *Landlord and Tenant Act* 1985, in certain cases, lettings of residential property imply a condition that the property is fit for human habitation and an undertaking by the landlord that it will remain so during the tenancy. While there are various issues that could be discussed in relation to section 8, its application depends on a low rent condition being satisfied and, with the limits being very low in the context of the modern residential letting market, the section is very rarely encountered in current practice. Therefore, it is not intended to consider it any more than to mention its existence.

1.7 THE DEMISED PROPERTY

As explained above, to be able to understand the obligations under the tenancy (whether on the landlord or tenant), in theory one first has to identify the property to which they relate. In practice, one generally finds that one has to refer to the whole of the tenancy since, particularly in the case of lettings of part of a property, it is quite rare that one can readily understand the extent of the demised property without reference to other provisions of the tenancy.

There are a number of ways in which a lease describes and defines the property it demises. Usually, in the case of written tenancies, having described the property demised, the tenancy uses a form of words to define them, e.g. 'the demised premises', and that definition should then appear throughout the lease so that, whenever one happens upon it, e.g. in the provisions setting out the obligations concerning the repair of the property, one can, in theory at least, understand exactly to what that obligation relates.

In the case of a letting of the whole of a property, the description of it should be straightforward. So, the lease may describe the demised property by reference to its address. It might also refer to a plan that indicates the whereabouts of the property and delineates the extent of it.

But even then the extent of the property demised might not be clear. For example, does it include the boundaries between it and neighbouring land?

Often, therefore, a simple general description of the land will not be enough and should be enhanced by some additional explanation. In the absence of that, one may not be able to fully understand the extent of the obligations concerning the form and condition of the property because of an uncertainty as to the extent of the property included in the demise. In those circumstances, one will have to try and interpret the lease to see what other guidance one can glean from it as to what it covers. In those circumstances, it may be necessary to seek legal advice.

In the case of property parts of which are let, the position regularly becomes more complicated. The various obligations as to the form and condition of the property should, in theory, collectively amount to a complete scheme for maintaining the property as a whole. While such complete schemes are often intended, frequently they are incomplete because the descriptions of the constituent parts of the property subject to different lettings do not, as it were, marry up. For example, it may not be clear whether the windows are included in the obligations of either the landlord or the tenant, or it might not be clear where the upper limit of a demise ends and the lower limit of the demise of property above starts – there could be a gap in between and it may not be clear whether that was intentional and whether the element of the property in between a lower and upper floor is to be retained by the landlord and therefore fall within its responsibility.

There are, however, various ways in which one can better understand the extent of the property demised where there are such problems of interpretation. For example, one could refer to a plan or there may be cases that have considered particular problems. The difficulty is that with each property being different and each lease often being different, while one can refer to cases on particular issues, they can be no more than a guide as to what a court might decide in any specific case; there can be no guarantee that the court would reach any particular decision. Some examples of such cases are set out below.

In addition, the position can be further complicated where the property is altered or added to. Where the lease is silent on the subject, perhaps referring only to the demised premises, obligations to repair the property could extend to additions to it. Where, however, the lease is referable to the property as it existed at the time the lease was entered into, then the obligations to repair are likely also to be so limited.

1.7.1 The plan

As mentioned above, there is often a plan annexed to the lease. Depending on the form of words used to refer to it, it might either assist in identifying the property demised with the words in the lease taking priority (e.g. 'for the purposes of identification only') or the plan may be more important than the words in the lease (e.g. 'more particularly delineated on the plan').

1.7.2 Examples of cases concerning the extent of the demise

Petersson v Pitt Place (Epsom) Ltd (2001)

In a case where both the landlord and the tenants could have been responsible for the repair of roof terraces, the Court of Appeal held that the tenants were because they were within the property demised to them.

Ibrahim v Dovecorn Reversions Ltd (2001)

In a case decided two months after *Petersson*, the judge concluded that the roof terrace was within the definition of 'main structure' and therefore the responsibility of the landlord. This exemplifies the principle that each case turns on its own facts, because, notwithstanding the decision in *Petersson*, the judge was only concerned to interpret the specific lease in issue.

Strandley Investments v Barpress (1987)

The lease demised all that:

> 'piece or parcel of ground with the messuages and buildings erected thereon situate and being on the South side of and Numbered 67, 69, 71, 73, 75, 77, 79 and 81 in Mortimer Street.'

The Court of Appeal decided that it was impossible to argue that that lease did not demise the roof of the buildings and the exterior walls.

Cockburn v Smith (1924)

By contrast with *Strandley Investments Ltd v Barpress*, in a case referred to in *Strandley* where the lease was of a top-floor flat and there were other flats in the property including another on the top floor, the roof was held not to be included in the demise to the tenant.

1.8 THE PARTIES AND DILAPIDATIONS CLAIMS

Having established the terms of the tenancy (see Chapter 2 for a consideration of frequently encountered covenants) and the property to which it relates, one will need to consider against whom the obligations of the tenancy could be enforced. One will also need to consider whether there are any steps that need to be taken and if so whether they must be taken within any time limit to ensure that someone is liable under the relevant obligations.

In practice, this exercise might and perhaps should be considered very early on because it may be that, in some circumstances, having identified the person(s) or company(ies) against whom the terms of the lease might be enforced, one establishes that any such action is inappropriate because the person/company is not financially worth pursuing, bearing in mind the cost and frequent uncertainty of pursuing a dilapidations claim.

In simple cases where the lease was made between a landlord and a tenant and neither have transferred their interest, the one can enforce obligations against the other.

Where the landlord or the tenant has transferred its interest, the position becomes more complex, particularly when the lease was entered into after the implementation of the *Landlord and Tenant (Covenants) Act* 1995 on 1 January 1996 (which might be said to offer greater protection to tenants than landlords, in terms of the enforceability of covenants). In the case of leases entered into before 1 January 1996, subject to the application of some provisions of the *Landlord and Tenant (Covenants) Act* 1995 in some circumstances, the original tenant will remain liable under its covenants even after the tenancy created by the lease has been assigned to someone else.

The position might also be complicated where, as often happens, obligations concerning the form and condition of the property are contained in licences, whether to assign or to alter the property. Although not free from doubt, one would imagine that, unless the obligations entered into (e.g. to be bound by the tenant covenants in a lease for the remainder of its duration or to reinstate alterations undertaken by the tenant) are expressed to be personal to the landlord or tenant, the benefit and burden of them will pass on a transfer of the landlord's or tenant's interest.

Friends Provident Life Office v British Railways Board (1996)

Where, as in this case, the tenant's interest has been assigned, the original tenant cannot be made liable for increased obligations agreed between the landlord and the assignee (unless the original tenant had consented to the change). The exception would be where the lease entered into by the original tenant envisaged the possibility of variation. That could arise where there was a provision banning alterations without first obtaining the landlord's consent or where there was no ban at all against alterations and the effect of alterations carried out by an assignee extended the property which was subject to, say, tenants' repairing obligations.

Metropolitan Properties Co (Regis) Ltd v Bartholomew (1996)

A surety is discharged from liability by any variation of the principal contract (the performance of which he has guaranteed) which may be agreed between the principal debtor and the creditor, without his consent, unless the variation is clearly insubstantial or it is self-evident without inquiry that it is one which cannot prejudice him.

RPH Ltd v Mirror Group (Holdings) Ltd (1993)

In the case of a lease entered into before 1 January 1996, where a tenant has assigned its interest, it usually has either an express or implied indemnity from the assignee that the assignee will pay the rent under the lease and otherwise comply with its obligations. If the lease is further assigned, the first assignee will have a similar indemnity from the further assignee. However, the tenant cannot require the first assignee to enforce the indemnity of which it has the benefit against the further assignee.

Wright v Dean (1948)

Although there is provision in the *Landlord and Tenant (Covenants) Act* 1995 for the landlord to obtain a release of its covenants when it assigns its interest (provided the requisite procedure is followed), in the case of leases entered into before 1 January 1996 the original landlord will remain liable under its covenants even after an assignment of its reversionary interest.

Estates Gazette Ltd v Benjamin Restaurants Ltd (1994)

It is well known that an assignee of the tenant's interest will be liable to the landlord for the 'tenant' covenants for so long as it remains in the position of tenant (i.e. until any further assignment), but leases often require assignees to enter into direct covenants with the landlord agreeing to comply with the obligations in the lease for the remainder of its term thereby putting the assignee into the same 'contractual' position as the original tenant.

Law of Property Act 1925, sections 141 and 142

Where a landlord has transferred its interest, the new landlord will be able to enforce the 'tenants' covenants under the lease (e.g. so could recover arrears of rent owed by the tenant to the landlord's predecessor – contrast that with tenancies entered into from 1 January 1996; see section 23(1) and (2) of the *Landlord and Tenant (Covenants) Act* 1995) and will be responsible for the performance of the 'landlord' covenants under the lease.

Duncliffe v Caerfelin Properties Ltd (1989)

As in this case, the assignee of a landlord's interest will not be responsible for damages for breaches of covenant by its predecessor.

Smith v Muscat (2003)

A tenant who had a claim for damages against a previous landlord could set off that claim against a claim by a successor to that landlord for rents owed by the tenant to the previous landlord where the right to collect those arrears of rent had passed to the successor.

Landlord and Tenant Act 1985, section 3

In the case of a dwelling, where the landlord's interest is assigned, written notice of the assignment is to be given to the tenant and, until it is, the 'old' landlord remains liable under the 'landlord' covenants. If there is a breach by the 'new' landlord and written notice of the assignment of the landlord's interest has not yet been given to the tenant, the 'new' landlord can be liable too.

Landlord and Tenant (Covenants) Act 1995

The *Landlord and Tenant (Covenants) Act* 1995 modifies the law in relation to liability under leases. It primarily benefits tenants who have entered into leases from 1 January 1996 but has some impact on the enforcement of covenants under leases entered into prior to that date.

Section 3 – The benefit and burden of the landlord and tenant covenants under a lease pass on an assignment of either the landlord or tenant's interest, but under section 23 the assignee of the landlord or tenant's interest does not take on any rights or liabilities under such covenants for any period prior to the assignment although the benefit of rights under the leases prior to the assignment can be transferred. So, for example, under a lease entered into after 1 January 1996, a successor landlord could not collect arrears of rent due to its predecessor unless the right to do so had been assigned to the new landlord – see the reference above to section 141 of the *Law of Property Act* 1925. The effect of section 3 applies to licences as well since it applies to covenants contained in collateral agreements.

Section 5 – On an assignment by a tenant of the tenancy created by a lease entered into after 1 January 1996, the tenant is released from its covenants, subject to the possibility of requiring the tenant to guarantee the performance, by the assignee, of the tenant covenants (see section 16) under what is known as an authorised guarantee agreement. Where a tenant is released, so is its guarantor (if any) – see section 24(2).

Sections 6 and 7 – Unlike the tenant who assigns its interest, when a landlord's interest under a tenancy created by a lease entered into after 1 January 1996 is assigned, the landlord may be released from its covenants, but only if the notice and court order based procedure in section 8 is satisfied.

Section 11 – Provision is made for what are known as 'excluded assignments', these being assignments in breach of covenant (e.g. where the landlord's prior permission was required but not obtained or where there is a ban on assignments) or where there is an assignment by operation of law (e.g. the grant of an underlease for a term longer than the remainder of the term of the lease). In such cases, among other things, the tenant will not be released from its covenants until an assignment which is not an excluded assignment takes place.

Section 16 – See section 5 above. Even if the former tenant is required to enter into an authorised guarantee agreement, any such agreement cannot extend the former tenant's liability beyond the period during which the term granted by the lease is vested in the assignee. Once the lease is further assigned, the former tenant is released completely from liability.

Section 17 – Where a former tenant remains liable for the tenant covenants under a lease (either because the lease was entered into before 1 January 1996 or because the former tenant under a lease entered into after that date was required to enter into an authorised guarantee agreement or because the lease was the subject of an excluded assignment), the former tenant cannot be made to pay any fixed amounts due under the lease unless, within six months of the amount becoming due, the landlord served an appropriate notice on the former tenant informing it of its liability to pay the amount(s) concerned. There is a similar scheme for guarantors to former tenants to a lease. In the context of dilapidations claims, such fixed amounts might arise when a landlord has entered the property and carried out works the cost of which can, under the lease, be passed on to the tenant (see Chapter 6, *Remedies*). Where a former tenant or its guarantor pays the amount(s) provided for by the required notice, under section 19 the former tenant or its guarantor (depending on who paid) can require the landlord to grant to it an overriding lease. The purpose of obtaining such a lease would be to enable the former tenant or its guarantor to take control of the property and, if possible, assign it so that its continuing liability can be kept in check.

Section 18 – Where a former tenant remains bound by the tenant covenants under the lease, it shall not be liable to pay any amount in respect of the covenant to the extent that the amount is referable to a variation (which the landlord could have refused) of the tenant covenants after the assignment.

Section 25 – Agreements seeking to avoid the effect of the *Landlord and Tenant (Covenants) Act* 1995 are void.

2
Frequently encountered covenants and lease provisions

In this chapter, the types of obligation and lease provision that are frequently encountered in dilapidations claims will be considered in greater detail. Included are obligations and provisions found in licences (e.g. to alter) that are frequently expressed to be part of the lease (e.g. to reinstate alterations) and enforceable as if they were (e.g. by forfeiture – see Chapter 6). The obligations and provisions will be considered from the point of view that they primarily affect the tenant, but the principles will apply (where appropriate, e.g. in relation to obligations to repair) to landlords as well. The options for (and restrictions on) enforcement are considered in Chapter 6, *Remedies*.

2.1 TO REPAIR

There are a number of ways in which a covenant to repair can be expressed. In simple terms, the obligation will be 'to repair' the property. Sometimes, however, the obligation appears to be qualified or that simple expression is modified.

For example, the obligation may be to 'put the property into repair'. Where such words are encountered, one might conclude that the intention was that the tenant would be obliged to carry out whatever work was required to bring the condition of the property up to a level that would be considered 'in repair'. In other words, the expression contemplates that the property is not in repair when the lease is entered into or it might fall out of repair and the tenant has to address that. Sometimes such covenants 'to put' property into repair are further modified such that it appears that there is a timeframe for doing so, e.g. by the use of words such as 'forthwith' or by reference to a specific date or a period of time. In the case of the former example, the obligation may require that the repairs are carried out within a reasonable time and, perhaps obviously, in relation to the latter example, the tenant will be in breach if it has not complied with the obligation by the date specified (although there is sometimes room for doubt about when the period begins and ends if the obligation is dependent on some other event occurring).

Alternatively, the obligation may be to 'keep in repair the property'. Such an expression adds little to the covenant to repair and, if the property is not in repair (whether when the lease is entered into or during the term of the lease), it still requires the tenant to put it into repair.

It is worth noting too that a covenant simply using the words 'to repair' implies 'to put in repair' and 'to keep in repair', both of which have just been considered.

In almost all cases, the obligation to repair is present whether or not the tenant is actually aware of disrepair. However, in some limited cases the obligation may be linked to the tenant being given or having notice of the disrepair. Naturally, if there is such a limitation, then the tenant (or landlord, if the obligation is on the landlord) will not be in breach unless notice has been given and requisite action not taken within any time limits (if there are any – sometimes the lease provides that the tenant may have two or three months to carry out the work). Covenants providing for the landlord to enter, carry out work and recover the cost from the tenant are considered in 2.7.

For obvious reasons one needs to identify and understand the covenant to repair and its extent (its extent may be limited in some way, e.g. by reference to a schedule of condition – see Chapter 3), but it is also necessary to do so because it is this covenant that is affected by section 18 of the *Landlord and Tenant Act* 1927 which is considered below at Chapter 6, *Remedies*.

For a more detailed discussion of the variations on the covenant to repair, see Dowding and Reynolds, chapter 14.

The covenant to repair carries with it an implied covenant not to destroy the subject matter of the covenant, in whole or in part.

Devonshire Reid Properties Ltd v Trenaman (1997)

In a case concerning enfranchisement issues and whether the landlord should receive compensation in the price to be paid to it for the loss of the ability to develop the roof of the property, the Lands Tribunal concluded that it should not because the landlord would not be able to give effect to any plans it might have had to do such work as to do so would break its covenant to repair the roof.

Hannon v 169 Queens Gate Ltd (2000)

The point made in *Devonshire Reid* was taken up, but in this case and having regard to the terms of the specific lease(s), the court concluded that the work proposed (which would have 'destroyed' the subject matter of the covenant) could proceed.

Unless the wording of the obligation to repair is extremely detailed and specific to the property (in the latter respect, unfortunately, it is not always the case that the lease has been drafted to cater for the specific property), it is sometimes unclear how far the covenant extends. That can be the case both in relation to the extent of the property covered by the obligation (which may be linked to identifying the extent of the property demised by the lease) and the extent of the work that can be undertaken.

2.1.1 Examples of cases concerning the extent of the property to which the obligation attaches

Grigsby v Melville (1974)

Unless the lease suggests otherwise, the property demised will extend to include the airspace above the property and the soil beneath, so, in a case where there was a cellar immediately beneath the property to which access could not be gained directly from the property but via neighbouring land, the cellar was held to be part of the property.

Davies v Yadegar (1990)

Where the demise of a top-floor flat included the roof, it included the airspace above too so that the tenant could alter the profile of the roof.

Cockburn v Smith (1924)

But where it is unclear whether or not the roof is demised, in the case of multi-let property, where the lease was of a top-floor flat and there were other flats in the property including another on the top floor, the roof was held not to be included in the demise to the tenant.

2.1.2 Examples of cases concerning the extent of the work required or permitted by the obligation

Brew Bros Ltd v Snax (Ross) Ltd (1970)

As this case illustrates, just because a lease contains a covenant to repair does not necessarily mean that all work to, apparently, restore the property to the condition it was once in would be 'repair' – it is a question of fact and degree. One must consider the particular property, the state it was in when the lease was granted and the terms of the lease, and then reach a conclusion as to whether the work said to be necessary can fairly be termed repair.

Holding & Management Ltd v Property Holding & Investment Trust plc (1990)

In greater detail than in *Brew Bros*, the court held that the proper approach was as follows:

> 'Thus the exercise involves considering the context in which the word "repair" appears in a particular lease and also the defect and remedial works proposed. Accordingly, the circumstances to be taken into account in a particular case under one or other of these heads will include some or all of the following: the nature of the property, the terms of the lease, the state of the property at the date of the lease, the nature and extent of the defect sought to be remedied, the nature, extent, and cost of the proposed remedial works, at whose expense the proposed remedial works are to be done, the value of the property and its

expected lifespan, the effect of the works on such value and lifespan, current building practice, the likelihood of a recurrence if one remedy rather than another is adopted, the comparative cost of alternative remedial works and their impact on the use and enjoyment of the property by the occupants. The weight to be attached to these circumstances will vary from case to case.

This is not a comprehensive list. In some cases there will be other matters properly to be taken into account. For example, as in the present case, where a design or construction fault has led to part of the property falling into a state of disrepair, and the proposed remedial works extend to other parts of the property, an important consideration will be the likelihood of similar disrepair arising in the other parts of the property if remedial work is not undertaken there also, and how soon such further disrepair is likely to arise.'

Creska Ltd v Hammersmith and Fulham London Borough Council (1998)

The property had underfloor heating equipment that required repair, the cost of which would be expensive. The tenant proposed to meet its obligation by installing night storage heaters that would be more efficient as well as cheaper. The court rejected the tenant's proposal.

Postel Properties Ltd v Boots the Chemist Ltd (1996)

The landlord, on the advice of its surveyor, replaced in sections the whole of the roof covering (and undertook related work at the same time to a better specification). Although it might have been possible to continue with patch repairs, in the main the court upheld the landlord's decision.

Ravenseft Properties Ltd v Davstone (Holdings) Ltd (1979)

The landlord took down stone cladding which had started to come away from the property and was dangerous and reinstalled it but added expansion joints that had not previously formed part of the property. The tenant contended that the expansion joints were installed to remedy what was described as an inherent defect; it was not a case that an element of the property had fallen into a worse condition than it had been in – it had been built like that. Consequently, the tenant contended that the work was not of repair and that it did not have to pay for its cost through the service charge. The court concluded that there was no concept that inherent defects could never be remedied under an obligation to repair.

Post Office v Aquarius Properties Ltd (1987)

If there is an inherent defect in a property, but it has not resulted in the subject matter of the obligation to repair falling out of repair, then there is no obligation to remedy the inherent defect. In any event, it may be possible to carry out repairs to the subject matter of the obligation to repair without having to remedy the inherent defect. Further, the work to be undertaken may in fact go beyond work of repair as a matter of fact and degree and the effect of the work could be to give back to the landlord something wholly different from that which it demised. In this case, the property had been so constructed that the basement was ankle-deep in water whenever the water table rose. While the problem that gave rise to this could have been cured in a number of ways, the court held that to do so would not be repair which the tenant was liable to carry out.

Gibson Investments Ltd v Chesterton plc (No. 1) (2002)

Where it is contended that the repair work should extend to eradicating the problem, rather than being limited to prophylactic measures, the cases establish, first, that the work will not be repair if it involves giving back to the landlord something wholly different from that which he demised, but, second, there will be circumstances in which such work can be repair even though it involves adding something to the property that was not there originally, as in *Ravenseft* and *Elmcroft*.

Elmcroft Developments Ltd v Tankersley-Sawyer (1984)

The basement flat suffered from severe damp that damaged the plaster on the walls. The landlord contended that it was sufficient for patching up repairs to be undertaken whenever the plaster was in such a condition that work was required. The problem could have been resolved once and for all by the insertion of a damp-proof course. The court concluded that the landlord's obligation required it to install the damp-proof course so that the problem was resolved once and for all and the landlord did not have to repetitively carry out what would be futile work.

Pembery v Lamdin (1940)

But an obligation to repair will not require the covenantor to carry out work the effect of which would be to create a different thing from that demised. The tenant required the landlord to carry out work that would give her waterproof protection in the cellar that would then be dry (it did not have such protection and was not dry). The court held that was not something on which the tenant could insist because the obligation on the landlord was to repair what was demised and not to give the tenant something which was not demised (i.e. a dry cellar).

Minja Properties Ltd v Cussins Property Group plc (1998)

Often there is an element of improvement to the property that is a consequence of repair work being carried out. Sometimes the opportunity is deliberately taken to upgrade the subject matter of the covenant at the time repair work is carried out. So, in this case where the property had been constructed with single glazed steel-framed windows, which were liable to corrosion, the court allowed, as a repair, the replacement of all the windows with aluminium double glazed units.

2.1.3 Examples of cases illustrating the approach of the courts to particular parts of a property

Before illustrating the approach of the courts to particular parts of a property, one must be reminded that one should treat reference to case law with caution. As has been made clear earlier in this book, each case turns on its own facts and a case cannot necessarily be relied upon as determinative of how the court would decide a specific problem.

One should also bear in mind the guidance set out later in this book as to the relevant considerations when ascertaining whether or not there is a breach of the lease and, if there is, what work should be done to remedy it.

Postel Properties Ltd v Boots the Chemist Ltd (1996)

Roofs (repair/replacement/improvements) – The landlord, on the advice of its surveyor, replaced in sections the whole of the roof covering (and undertook related work at the same time to a better specification). Although it might have been possible to continue with patch repairs, in the main the court upheld the landlord's decision.

Sun Life Assurance plc v Thales Tracs Ltd (2001)

Roofs (including asbestos roofing sheets and tiles) – Some of the roofs under consideration were constructed of corrugated asbestos sheeting and another was constructed of asbestos tiles laid like conventional slates. There were, before the court, two options for repairing the defects to the roofs. One option (the landlord's), for which it was common ground, would provide an adequate repair and the tenant's recommendation, which *might* produce an adequate repair. There was no evidence before the judge that it would be possible to apply the tenant's solution to one of the roofs, it being outside the tenant's surveyor's expertise to say whether it was possible. The judge was left with no alternative but to hold that the landlord's suggestion, that the roof in question should be entirely overclad with profiled steel sheet, was the appropriate method of repair.

Riverside Property Investments Ltd v Blackhawk Automotive (2004)

Roofs (including asbestos roofing sheets) – Often the covenantor has the freedom to choose between two appropriate solutions: repair or replacement. The case concerned asbestos cement roof sheets and the method of attaching them.

> 'On the evidence, the repairs carried out by the defendant had been sufficient to comply with the covenant. The continued presence of asbestos in the original roof sheets that had not been replaced could not be a reason to contend that the defendant had breached its repairing obligation. There was no evidence to suggest that the manner of carrying out the repairs was in breach of covenant. The decision to use topfix fasteners could not be

criticised, and their installation by specialist roofing contractors also did not constitute a breach of covenant.'

Elite Investments Ltd v TI Bainbridge Silencers Ltd (1986)

Roofs (repair or replacement/new materials) – In a case where the court concluded that replacement of the roof was within the covenant to repair, there was debate about the effect of the proposed new roof utilising more modern materials. The court held that:

> 'it is not that the roof is going to be very different. It is a new material, but that is just taking advantage of better materials that are now on the market. It does not really alter the basic structure of the building and, after all, this is quite a simple building, it is not some complex structure such as [was considered in *Post Office v Aquarius Properties Ltd*]. This is a relatively simple building and the roof will not be largely changed simply because it has got a roof looking similar to the existing roof but made of modern materials. Further, it seems largely irrelevant, because the old material is available and costs the same. Counsel placed the greatest emphasis on the cost; it is totally disproportionate, he said, to the value of the building in repair. I have already dealt with that going through the cases, and in my judgment that is a false point. What has to be compared in this connection in determining whether you have got a repair or not, is not the value of the resulting building with the new roof but what it will cost you to do away with the building altogether and build a new one, or substantially build a new one. Then he said, having looked at the factors no reasonable landlord would do it. That again is not the test, if I may respectfully say so; it is a question of whether the tenants have undertaken to do what is done and what is the true meaning of the covenant. So my conclusion on that, as is evident from now, is that this is a repair or replacement of part within the meaning of the covenant. It is not a different thing. It will simply be an industrial building with a new roof. The consequence is that I find that the case for damages in relation to Unit 1 in the sum I mentioned of £84,364 is established.'

Minja Properties Ltd v Cussins Property Group plc (1998)

Windows/window frames – Often when work is carried out there is an element of improvement to the property that is a consequence of repair work being carried out, sometimes because the opportunity arising from the need to carry out some work is used to make some improvements. In this case the property had been constructed with single glazed steel-framed windows which were liable to corrosion. The court allowed, as a repair, the replacement of all the windows with aluminium double glazed units.

Reston Ltd v Hudson (1990)

Windows/window frames – It was discovered that many of the timber window frames were defective and required to be replaced. The judge noted that, for aesthetic reasons, it was desirable that one would either repair the defective ones with similar material or replace the lot; one would not replace some of them with different material, leaving other window frames of the original material. The landlords had taken the view that the time had now come when it would be appropriate to replace all the timber windows. If they did that under one substantial contract it would be considerably cheaper than it would be if it were left to individual tenants to do it from time to time. Despite a reference in the demise of the flat to 'glass windows therein', the judge came to the conclusion that the external windows were not included in the demise. It appeared that there were internal glass windows in the flats and this, together with other features of the lease, satisfied him that the external windows were not included. The landlord's repairing covenant covered, among other things, 'windows and structures of the estate other than those for which the lessee is responsible'. If the external windows were not included in the demise, the tenant was clearly not so responsible. The service charge payable by the tenants covered 'costs and expenses incurred by the lessor', including the matters for which the lessor was responsible under the repairing covenants.

Ravenseft Properties Ltd v Davstone (Holdings) Ltd (1979)

Cladding/expansion joints – As noted in 2.1.2, the inclusion of expansion joints not previously present could be within the covenant to repair (as it related to cladding).

Gibson Investments Ltd v Chesterton plc (No. 1) (2002)

Steel frame building and corrosion – There were three options for treatment of the steel frame. But which should be carried out? The judge said:

> 'First, in my judgment, the first scheme, if carried out, unlike the second or third schemes, would not result in the building being in repair even at the moment that the works were completed. The continued presence of laminating rust in areas adjacent to places where the laminated rust has caused cracking would, in my view, constitute disrepair. The rusting is substantial, and the rusting that the second scheme would involve removing would be in runs that have already caused cracking. If there is a run of laminated rust that has not caused cracking, there would be no need to deal with it under the second scheme. The fact that the structural function of the steel frame is not currently under threat does not, in my view, call this conclusion into question. It appears to me that the fact that laminating rusting has already caused significant cracking in places means that one cannot say that the building is in repair if there are runs of laminating rusting that have caused the cracking.
>
> Second, it seems to me that it would be inappropriate not to carry out the extra remedial work involved in the second scheme over the first scheme at the same time as repairing the cracks in the stonework and brickwork. In this connection, I consider that the present case is comparable with cases such as [*Elmcroft Developments Ltd v Tankersley-Sawyer*]. In that case, the landlord was obliged, under his repairing covenant, to install a damp-proof course to eliminate rising damp, rather than to carry on replacing the plaster as and when it became soft. Much the same can be said about the first scheme, as against the second scheme or (if it works) the third scheme. The effect of implementing the second or third schemes (costing about £1m at the most) should obviate the need for any

significant work to the exterior walls for the remaining 11 or so years of the lease, and possibly much longer than that. The first scheme works, if carried out, costing a little over £400,000, will probably have to be repeated some three times before the lease ends.'

Gibson Investments Ltd v Chesterton plc (No. 2) (2003)

Air conditioning – The defendant landlord granted the claimant tenant a new lease for office property. A clause in the lease provided that the tenant was responsible for the repair, renewal or replacement of the air-conditioning system. It was common ground that the original system was inadequate and that, when the tenant replaced it, the replacement would fall within the terms of the lease. Two replacement systems were available. The one chosen by the tenant resulted in the relocation of various elements of the system, thereby creating more floor space. The tenant contended that the creation of this additional space amounted to an improvement, and it applied to the court for a declaration to that effect. The landlord maintained that works of repair could not constitute improvements, and that the work carried out merely represented the tenant's obligation under the lease. The court held, allowing the tenant's claim, that the obligation to repair the system was an obligation to replace the system (if repair was insufficient) with something similar, and, if possible, included locating it in the same, or a similar, position. On the facts of the case, the tenant could have installed the new system in the same position as its predecessor, but it chose not to do so. Relocating the system was not, therefore, necessary for the purposes of the repair. The installation of the new air-conditioning system had discharged the tenant's repairing obligation, but it had also altered the property so as to increase the letting space. That alteration required consent under the terms of the lease. Upon the grant of such consent, the work would be classed as an improvement to be disregarded on rent review on the assumption that the obligation under the original repair clause had been met.

Post Office v Aquarius Properties Ltd (1987)

Damp/water penetration – The defective construction of the basement led to water being present in the basement.

The defective parts of the property were in the same condition as when constructed, i.e. their condition had not deteriorated so they were not then in disrepair. The court would not require the tenant to carry out the work necessary to make the property waterproof.

Elmcroft Developments Ltd v Tankersley-Sawyer (1984)

Damp/damp-proof courses – It will not always be the case that just because there is no damp-proof course in place already there is no obligation to install one. One must consider whether the presence of damp has caused disrepair (in *Post Office v Aquarius Properties Ltd* it did not). Just because a property or part of it is damp does not mean that there is disrepair. If there is damp which causes disrepair, then if it is not realistic to repair the damp affected part of the property without also curing the design defect, then the installation of a damp-proof course could be within the obligation to repair.

Eyre v McCracken (2001)

Damp/damp-proof courses – Unlike *Elmcroft* the court held that the installation of a damp-proof course would not be within the covenant to repair. However, the lease in this case was short and the repairing obligation was on the tenant, unlike in *Elmcroft* where the position was the reverse.

Quick v Taff-Ely Borough Council (1985)

Damp/condensation – The residential tenant had to endure dismal conditions as a result of condensation caused by the manner in which the windows had been constructed and the inadequate central heating system, but the court concluded that, since the property had been built according to the regulations and standards of the time and the problems were not the result of damage to the part of the property that had led to their creation, there was no disrepair.

This case should be contrasted with *Welsh v Greenwich London Borough Council* (2000) considered in Chapter 4, *Have the covenants been broken?*, where the covenant to repair was not broken but a covenant to maintain the property in good condition was.

2.2 TO DECORATE

Quite apart from decoration that may be required to meet any obligation to repair, most leases also contain a separate obligation to decorate the property.

Where the lease does not contain such a covenant, one will be reliant on the covenant to repair. Just because, however, the property may be in a poor decorative condition does not mean that it is out of repair and that decoration needs to be undertaken to meet the covenant to repair. However, under the test in *Proudfoot v Hart* (see Chapter 4, *Have the covenants been broken?*), if the decorative standard falls below the standard that would be accepted by a reasonably minded tenant who would be of the type likely to take a lease of the property, then decoration may be required under the repairing covenant.

2.2.1 No express covenant to decorate

Proudfoot v Hart (1890)

'"Good tenantable repair" is such repair as having regard to the age, character and locality of the [property] as would make [it] reasonably fit for the occupation of a reasonably minded tenant of the class who would be likely to take [it] … [the property] need not be put into the same condition as when the tenant took [it], [it] need not be put in perfect repair.'

Irvine v Moran (1991)

The question in this case was: Did an implied obligation to keep the structure and exterior of a residential property include an obligation to decorate?

- Yes, in relation to the exterior because that would involve a 'degree of protection against the elements and against the processes of rot and the like'.

- No, in relation to the purely decorative interior unless work was necessary to fulfil the obligation to repair.

2.2.2 Express covenant to decorate

Gemmell v Goldsworthy (1942)

This was an Australian case. An express covenant to decorate within a specified, recurring, period was absolute and unconditional but the covenant to repair would still apply and decoration in the middle of any such period could still be required if that was the effect of meeting the obligation to repair.

Simmons v Dresden (2004)

As this case suggests, it does not matter, in terms of assessing performance, whether the property needs decorating – if the covenant says one must decorate and it is not carried out, there is a breach.

The covenant may dictate how the covenant is to be met, i.e. it may prescribe the colour scheme or standard of materials to be used or it may make it a condition that, prior to decoration being carried out, the choice of colour and/or materials be approved by the landlord or its surveyor. What happens in such circumstances very much depends on the specific wording of the lease. The covenant may state that the landlord or its surveyor may not unreasonably withhold consent or it may be that the appointment of the surveyor operates as a condition precedent so that the obligation to decorate does not bite until then.

Law of Property Act 1925, section 147

By contrast with the entitlement to seek relief from forfeiture where a notice is served under section 146 of the *Law of Property Act* 1925, after a notice is served on a tenant relating to the internal decorative repairs to a house or other building, under section 147 of the Act the tenant may apply to the court for relief, and if, having regard to all the circumstances of the case (including in particular the length of the term or interest remaining unexpired), the court is satisfied that the notice is unreasonable, it may, by order, wholly or partially relieve the tenant from liability for such repairs. In practice, one rarely sees the entitlement under section 147 operated. In part that is due to the exceptions to it, but if one can make an application, it could be of advantage to a tenant because the outcome could be to relieve the tenant altogether from an obligation to perform the covenant in relation to internal decorative repair.

2.3 TO YIELD UP

The obligation to yield up the property to the landlord at the end of the lease often covers two areas:

- to give vacant possession; and
- to do so with the property being in repair and otherwise on the basis that the obligations in the lease have been met.

The problems arising where the tenant leaves others in the property at the end of the lease are not of concern in this book. However, if there are subtenants in the property (whether with the landlords consent or not), the terms of the subtenancy could have an impact on the amount of damages the landlord could claim against the, by then, former tenant for dilapidations, since it is possible that the subtenants are themselves subject to full obligations as to the form and condition of the property which the landlord can enforce against them thereby resulting in an assertion that the landlord's damages against the former tenant are not as great as they might otherwise have been or have even been extinguished.

However, where the tenant leaves its belongings in the property, the effect of that could be that it is deemed not to have delivered up vacant possession. Such belongings, in the context of a dilapidations claim could include items of furniture that the tenant should have removed when it left the property. By leaving them in situ, the landlord may have to remove them and in doing so incur a cost that it could claim from the former tenant. There is sometimes a debate about the legal 'nature' of such belongings because in some cases it might be argued that, by their very nature or by virtue of the manner in which they are in the property, they are fixtures which may (or may not) be something that the tenant has to remove. Fixtures are considered in 2.6.

If the tenant fails to deliver up the property to the landlord in repair, that can give rise to a separate claim against the tenant in addition (as is likely in such circumstances) to a claim that the general covenant to repair has been broken.

Arguments on whether a tenant has yielded up possession are set to continue because there is no set procedure to ensure that property is delivered up.

John Laing Construction Ltd v Amber Pass Ltd (2004)

The claimant tenant held a lease from the defendant landlord. The lease contained a break clause that was exercisable by the tenant upon giving six months' notice expiring at the end of the 15th year of the term. The break clause provided that, upon the payment of the equivalent of 12 months' rent and 'upon yielding up of the entirety of the demised premises' at the expiry of the notice, the term would cease and determine. Although the tenant had vacated the property, it had left in place a number of security barriers and security guards because of a continuing and serious problem of vandalism and trespass. The landlord contended that, by reason of the security barriers, the presence of the security guards and the failure to offer up the keys, the tenant had not formally yielded up the property, and the lease therefore continued. The tenant issued proceedings seeking a declaration that the lease had determined.

The court held that the lease had determined that there was no prescribed form or procedure for 'yielding up'. In the case of a unilateral termination of a lease, the task of the court was to look objectively at what had occurred and to determine whether:

- a clear intention had been manifested by the party seeking a termination to effect such termination; and

- the landlord could, if it so wished, occupy the property without difficulty or objection.

Retention of the keys did not signify an intention by the tenant to assert any rights in respect of the property. The continued presence of security staff and the barriers did not create any hindrance to the landlord. The tenant had plainly and obviously manifested a desire to terminate the lease.

2.4 NOT TO ALTER

Many leases contain provisions concerning alterations to the property. In the absence of such provisions, it would seem to be the case that the tenant is not precluded from altering the property, provided, of course, that in doing so, it does not break one or more of the covenants that do exist.

Where there are provisions in the lease concerning alterations, they usually follow a similar format. The simplest of provisions simply ban alterations. More often, the lease permits alterations of certain types or to certain parts of the property but only in certain circumstances. The more comprehensive of leases might ban alterations of a certain type (e.g. to the structure), permit certain types of alterations provided the landlord's written consent is first obtained and then allow any other types of alteration without qualification.

Landlord and Tenant Act 1927, section 19(2)

In all leases, whether made before or after the commencement of the *Landlord and Tenant Act* 1927 (25 March 1928), containing a covenant condition or agreement against the making of improvements without licence or consent, such covenant condition or agreement shall be deemed, notwithstanding any express provision to the contrary, to be subject to a proviso that such licence or consent is not to be unreasonably withheld; but the proviso does not preclude the right of the landlord to require as a condition of such licence or consent the payment of a reasonable sum in respect of any damage to or diminution in the value of the property or any neighbouring property belonging to the landlord, and of any legal or other expenses properly incurred in connection with such licence or consent nor, in the case of an improvement which does not add to the letting value of the holding, does it preclude the right to require as a condition of such licence or consent, where such a requirement would be reasonable, an undertaking on the part of the tenant to reinstate the property in the condition in which they were before the improvement was executed.

If the lease prohibits alterations, then section 19(2) of the *Landlord and Tenant Act* 1927 will not assist; it only applies where there is a qualified covenant such that alterations can take place, but only with consent. In practice most modern leases already contain words reflecting the condition introduced by the subsection.

Where alterations are permitted, either by the lease itself or, more often, by a licence for alterations, it is sometimes the case that the relevant covenant will require that the property is reinstated at some later point (usually by the end of the lease) to the form and condition it was in before the alterations were carried out. Such requirements are considered in the next section. If alterations are prohibited, then it is suggested that it must follow that the tenant can be obliged to reinstate the property by an injunction (an order requiring someone to do or not to do something) and/or there could be a claim for damages if the tenant does not do so.

2.5   TO REINSTATE

It is sometimes the case that the lease or, more likely, a licence for alterations will contain a covenant that the property is reinstated at some later point (usually by the end of the lease) to the form and condition it was in before the alterations were carried out. When and to what extent such a covenant will operate will, as usual, depend on the precise wording of the obligation.

2.5.1   Landlord and Tenant Act 1927, section 19(2)

The effect of section 19(2) of the *Landlord and Tenant Act* 1927 is set out in section 2.4 'Not to alter'. It will be noted that where the lease permits alterations with consent, where such a requirement would be reasonable, the landlord can require an undertaking on the part of the tenant to reinstate the property in the condition in which it was before the improvement was executed.

In simple terms, the effect of the usual reinstatement covenant will be to require the tenant to remove whatever was introduced to the property and put back whatever was removed and make good any damage caused to the property as a result of the alterations and their reinstatement. It would seem, however, that immaterial changes to the original form and condition of the property would be acceptable.

It may not always be possible to achieve complete reinstatement thereby creating an issue as to the enforceability of the obligation.

Sturke v SW Edwards Ltd (1971)

So, using this case as an example, if reinstatement cannot be achieved because planning permission is required and, having been applied for, refused, it would seem that the tenant cannot avoid responsibility to the landlord who will have a potential claim for damages against the tenant. That is particularly the case if, as will often be the case in current times, the lease or licence was entered into after the planning legislation came into effect, so that the possibility of planning problems could have been contemplated by the parties.

Camden Theatre v London Scottish Properties Ltd (1984)

Or, there may be alternative materials to those originally used and which might, for example, be cheaper. In such a case where the original gold leaf decorated mouldings could have been replaced by gold painted ones, the court accepted the tenant's contentions that for the reinstatement obligation to be met in circumstances where the gold leaf mouldings were important to its use of the property, the gold painted mouldings were unacceptable.

Vural v Security Archives Ltd (1990)

While the court accepted that the relevant part of the property (a factory floor) should be reinstated to its previous material (wood rather than the lino the landlord proposed), it is clear that where the substitute material would meet the functional use to which the property is put, then alternative material could be permitted.

It is not always the case that the obligation to reinstate arises automatically. It could be the case that a landlord might want the tenant to leave the alterations in place. Therefore, the landlord will frequently reserve to itself the option to require the tenant to reinstate the property. Thus, many reinstatement obligations depend on the landlord having given notice to the tenant.

Where there is a notice provision in relation to reinstatement, then, since it must be the case that the tenant must have the ability to carry out the necessary work, if the clause does not make the position clear, one would assume that the notice will have to be given before the lease comes to an end because, once it has, the tenant no longer has an entitlement to remain at the property and will not be able to carry out work unless some specific arrangement for access has been entered into (e.g. a licence or, perhaps, a short lease if appropriate excluded from the protection of Part II of the *Landlord and Tenant Act 1954*, which can give security of tenure to a business tenant). However, it has been suggested that, unless there is a contractual provision as to the time by which a notice to reinstate must be given, it could be given at any time prior to the expiry of the lease even if that does not allow the tenant time to carry out the work.

Scottish Mutual Assurance Society Ltd v British Telecommunications plc (1994)

It has been suggested that if the landlord were to give its notice at a time when the tenant cannot comply before the lease expires, the tenant might be able to have a reasonable time to stay on at the property for the purpose of doing them.

While the concept of the tenant remaining in the property resolves the difficulty about late notice to reinstate being given by the landlord, it is not clear what the terms of occupation would be.

The principle that a licence to continue in occupation could come about, could lead to the contention that notice could be given after the end of the term of the lease, but that must be unlikely to be a correct analysis.

Westminster City Council v HSBC Bank plc (2003)

A schedule of dilapidations can include the requisite notice of the landlord's requirement that the tenant reinstate the property.

2.6 TO MAINTAIN FIXTURES/TO REMOVE FIXTURES/NOT TO REMOVE FIXTURES

Wherever fixtures are attached to the property, they may well form part of the property and therefore be within any obligation to repair the property. However, if that were always the case, one could not easily make sense of covenants to repair, say, the property and the landlord's fixtures. Such wording is not unusual. It would suggest, therefore, that fixtures in situ when the lease is entered into might have some characteristic other than being part of the principal demise. Such distinctions may be relevant if the lease does not demise the whole of the property but only part.

Boswell v Crucible Steel Co (1925)

In a case where the tenant covenanted to repair the interior of the demised property and the landlord's fixtures and the majority of the walls were, as a result of the type and size of the property, largely of glass, while in some circumstances 'windows' might be a fixture (as the landlord contended), here they were held to be a part of the structure of the property itself, not just a part of the interior.

If the item concerned is effectively part of the property, then it will not really be a fixture. But, where the item is indeed a fixture, a greater problem arises if the tenant has introduced it to the property. Arguments arise as to the standard of condition to which the items should be maintained (is the tenant obliged to repair them at all?), whether they can be removed by the tenant (before or at the end of the lease), what happens if they are damaged during removal or damage is caused to the property during their removal or what happens if the tenant is obliged to remove them and does not.

If the item is a chattel (i.e. personal property) belonging to the tenant, there is rarely any issue about the position – it is generally entirely up to the tenant as to what it does with them. However, if the tenant were to leave them at the property at the end of the lease, it could give rise to a damages claim by the landlord for failing to deliver up possession.

If the item is a fixture, then it is treated effectively as being part of the land. But there are some fixtures that a tenant can remove, particularly by the end of the term of the lease. These are known as 'tenant's fixtures'. Those fixtures that should not be removed by the tenant are known as 'landlord's fixtures'.

It will often be essential to understand the difference between the two categories so as to be able to understand the obligations of the tenant, particularly at the end of the lease.

To do so, one has to consider the manner in which the fixture is attached to the land.

If the item has not been attached to the property, that is a good indication that it remains a chattel. If it has been attached to the property, even to a limited extent, that could be an indication that it has become a fixture.

If an item rests on the property by its own weight, it is quite likely to be a chattel, even though it might be quite substantial (e.g. a shed). Equally, just because it does rest on the ground by its own weight will not always mean that the item is a chattel (e.g. heavy flagstones forming, say, a patio).

Where an item is attached to the property, one should consider whether it can be removed without doing appreciable damage to the property to which it is attached or to itself. If it cannot be removed without causing such damage, that is an indicator that the item may well be a fixture.

But the extent to which the item is attached to the property is not, of itself, the determining factor as to whether or not it is a fixture. One also has to consider the reason it was attached.

In this respect, if an item is attached for the purpose of achieving some permanent alteration or improvement to the property, it is more likely that it has become a fixture. Generally a domestic washing machine will be attached to the property so as to improve one's quality of use of the property, but while it is so attached, it is more likely to be removable (although the plumbing to which it is attached might not) often without damaging either itself or the property, so would objectively be considered to be a chattel.

2.6.1 Examples of cases illustrating the approach to items and whether or not they are fixtures

TSB Bank plc v Botham (1996)

Although one must continue to remember that each case turns on its own facts, in this particular case the following items were held to be fixtures:

- Bathroom fittings: in every case in which a bath had been fitted or built into the bathroom, the bath would have become a fixture and its taps would, on the face of it, follow suit. Very special evidence would be needed to justify a conclusion that although the bath was a fixture, its taps remained chattels. They were all fixtures.

- Fitted kitchen units: the evidence of photographs and common knowledge of the nature of fitted kitchen units justified the conclusion that the units installed in the flat had become fixtures.

The following were held not to have become fixtures:

- Fitted carpets and curtains: carpets, whether or not fitted, and curtains lacked the quality of permanency that was to be expected of articles that had become in the eye of the law part of the property.

- Light fittings: there was no admissible evidence to justify a conclusion that the light fittings had become fixtures.

- Gas fires: the only connection between the gas fires and the property was a gas pipe. Apart from that link, which was essential if they were to be used as gas fires, nothing secured the gas fires other than their own weight.

- White goods: the degree of annexation was slight – no more than was needed to allow normal use. They could be bought separately, by instalments, when ownership did not pass immediately. Disconnection could be done without damage to the fabric of the property and normally without difficulty.

Young v Dalgety (1987)

In a case which concerned a rent review clause and the impact of fixtures on it, light fittings which consisted of fluorescent tubes contained in glass boxes fixed securely to the plaster of the ceiling and floor covering being carpeting fixed to the floor by gripper rods, such rods being fixed to the floor with pins which were themselves attached to the carpet (the rods were laid on a screed floor) were both found to be tenant's fixtures. (This should be contrasted with *TSB Bank plc v Botham* where the carpets were cut to size and held in place by gripper rods yet held not to be fixtures.)

2.6.2 Carpets

Carpets often cause difficulties in the context of claims concerning dilapidations.

In many dilapidations claims, the costs of putting the carpets into repair (which typically means renewing them) can make up a significant proportion of the total value. Disputes often occur over whether the carpets belong to the landlord or are the tenant's chattels (see *TSB Bank plc v Botham* and *Young v Dalgety* above for a more detailed discussion of this).

In the absence of specific direction in the lease, it is necessary to consider the permanency with which the carpets have become annexed to the building. Carpets that are physically glued to the floors are probably fixtures that cannot be readily removed at the end of the term. If so, the tenant may become responsible for repairing or renewing them as demanded by the repair covenants. Conversely, where the carpet is merely held in place by carpet grippers, then it is unlikely to have become annexed and should be treated like other tenant's chattels.

Most modern offices are now specified with carpet tiles that are affixed with tackifier and are designed to be readily raised and moved about. As such, they are merely chattels. Even if they are provided by the landlord at the outset of the lease, they will not be subject to lease provisions that only refer to the demise. Unless, therefore, the lease explains how the landlord's possessions are to be looked after, the tenant is entitled to do as it wishes with these tiles and could merely remove them at the end of the lease.

Where leases are silent on the presence of carpets, this interpretation may not be representative of the intentions of the parties at the outset of the lease. After all, if a landlord has spent a large sum on providing carpets at the beginning of the lease, it is unlikely to wish to give them away for free. There may be compelling evidence to suggest that it was the intention of the parties to treat the carpets as the landlord's fixture. One should bear in mind, however, that when the court is considering the interpretation of the lease, it will not generally consider documents and events beyond that. Therefore, even if there is some evidence outside the lease as to what the parties intended in relation to carpets, there is no guarantee that this will be considered by the court.

As a result of these problems, and because many landlords provide property for let with carpets, many modern leases specifically confirm that carpets are part of the tenant's demise. The effect of this is to confirm that, irrespective of whether the carpets are fixtures or chattels, any lease provision that relates to the demise also relates to these.

2.6.3 Removal of fixtures

If an item introduced to the property has become part and parcel of it, then it can never be removed. But if an item has retained its characteristics as a fixture, then if it is a landlord's fixture it cannot be removed (this includes fixtures introduced by the tenant to replace existing landlord fixtures), whereas if it is a tenant's fixture it can.

In view of the similarity of outcome if an item has become part of the property or a landlord's fixture, one only needs to consider whether a fixture is a tenant's fixture.

To be a tenant's fixture the item must:

- have been attached to the property by or on behalf of the tenant;
- be a trade, decorative or domestic or agricultural fixture; and
- have been fixed with the intention of removing it when the tenant wished.

In the case of commercial property, one will mainly be concerned with the first category: trade fixtures are items that the tenant has introduced to enable it to carry on its trade or business at the property.

However, even if an item is a tenant's fixture, it may not be capable of removal since the lease may prohibit it.

Assuming, however, that there is no such limitation, there are other issues to consider in respect of the timing of the removal, since, on the face of it, a tenant can only do so during the continuance of the tenancy (there are some exceptions in the case of others, e.g. mortgagees of tenant's fixtures). Therefore, on forfeiture the right to remove is lost on peaceable re-entry or until judgment for possession (where forfeiture has been by way of proceedings). On surrender, the right to remove will also have been lost, unless the tenant has taken a new tenancy. Where the lease simply expires, whether by effluxion of time or the expiry of a notice to quit (or, it is submitted, a break notice), the right to remove would also generally be lost.

But the tenant does not have to remove tenant's fixtures, unless the lease (or a licence for alterations) directly or indirectly requires it. However, the decision not to remove such fixtures does not mean that they should be left in anything other than repair and where a tenant lawfully leaves fixtures at the property at the end of the lease, it could be exposed to a claim for damages if they have been left out of repair.

Whereas, if the tenant has introduced fixtures when it ought not to have done or has failed to remove fixtures when it should have done, the tenant will be exposed to a claim for damages (in the latter case, for introducing them in the first place). Equally, if the tenant removes fixtures it ought to have left in situ, it will be exposed to a claim in damages (if the landlord becomes aware of an intention to unlawfully remove fixtures before they have been removed, then it could seek an injunction preventing removal).

If the tenant has an obligation to remove fixtures or is entitled to do so and in doing so causes damage, then it is exposed to a claim by the landlord unless it makes good.

Mancetter Developments Ltd v Garmanson Ltd and Givertz (1986)

The liability to make good the damage, or to repair the injury the property may sustain by the act of removal of tenant's fixtures, must, in so far as it is a liability at common law and not under a contract, be the liability of the person who removes the fixtures, and not of the person, if different, who originally installed the fixtures and left them there. The liability to make good the damage is a condition of the tenant's right to remove tenant's fixtures; therefore, removal of the fixtures without making good the damage, being in excess of the tenant's right of removal, is waste, actionable in tort, just as much as removal by the tenant of a landlord's fixture, which the tenant has no right to remove, is waste. The filling of screw holes or nail holes where a fixture is removed which has been screwed or nailed to a wall may be a matter de minimis. But the leaving of holes, such as those in question in this case, affected the structure and was not a matter of mere decoration.

2.7 TO REPAIR ON NOTICE

Effectively an extension to the remedies otherwise available to a landlord, these days many leases contain an obligation on the tenant to allow the landlord and its representatives access to the property to inspect its condition and, if appropriate, to then serve a schedule of work to be done to comply with the covenants in the lease, all under the threat that the landlord will undertake the work if the tenant fails to and will then be entitled to recover the cost of doing so from the tenant. Such clauses mostly provide that the tenant be given a minimum period of time to carry out the works set out in the schedule. With the benefits highlighted by *Jervis v Harris* (see below), the remedy can be very useful to a landlord. However, there are some potential practical problems, for example:

- the landlord will have to forward-fund the cost of the works; and
- if the landlord needs to recover the cost from the tenant, it should make sure that the tenant has the means to pay (a tenant that has failed to comply with its obligations under the lease may – and only, may – be experiencing financial difficulties).

Covenants to repair on notice are distinct from the general covenants to repair, which frequently do not involve the concept of notice being given for the purposes of operating the covenant.

Jervis v Harris (1996)

If covenants to repair on notice are operated, as in this case, they can also give rise to the collateral benefit of not triggering the requirement to comply with the *Leasehold Property (Repairs) Act* 1938. It is also considered that section 18(1) of the *Landlord and Tenant Act* 1927 will not apply either. Both are considered in relation to the question of remedies in Chapter 6.

Of course, the landlord may only safely operate such a remedy if it complies strictly with the letter of the lease. Therefore, if notice in a particular form or of a particular duration is required or if certain conditions must be satisfied, the landlord must ensure compliance. Otherwise a trespass may be committed. Moreover, it is not open to the landlord to undertake works that are not within the obligation of the tenant and/or were not the subject of the notice that will have preceded the entry. If there is more than one scheme of work that might be undertaken, the landlord should choose that which is reasonable in the circumstances; if the landlord elected to undertake, say, the highest specification of work when another more economic scheme would be reasonable, it will be at risk of either no recovery or a shortfall in recovery of the cost incurred. Further, the landlord could find itself liable under some of the tenant's obligations if it fails to give effect to them when carrying out the tenant's work. If these problems were not enough, the landlord could also be faced with the practical (and legal) problems of sourcing necessary services – it may not follow that just because the landlord is entitled under the lease to enter the property to carry out work in default of the tenant having done so that it can simply make use of the tenant's supply of water and electricity, etc. That said, if the landlord is carrying out the work the tenant should have done and the tenant would have made use of such supplies, one could argue that the landlord could too.

Indeed, there could be significant problems for the landlord if there is no such clause and it chooses to enter anyway to carry out works that are within the obligation of the tenant; it could find itself being sued for trespass and, to rub salt into the wounds, may not be able to recover all or some of the costs it incurs in carrying out the work. If the landlord did seek to enter and carry out work in this manner, unlike a *Jervis v Harris* case, the 1938 Act and 1927 Act would probably apply.

Hammersmith & Fulham London Borough Council v Creska (No. 2) (2000)

If a tenant is served with notice by the landlord but then declines to give access, the landlord might have no alternative but to seek an injunction against the tenant forcing it to allow the landlord to carry out the work. As illustrated by this case, an injunction will not always be granted. The tenant had done a large amount of underfloor heating work, but not to one of the floors because, it said, to do so would be very disruptive to its business; it made provision for the work to be done at the end of the lease and set aside funds to cover the cost. The landlord's request for an injunction was declined. In most cases, however, one would expect the court to grant an injunction.

2.8 TO COMPLY WITH STATUTES

There are many pieces of legislation that, although primarily imposing obligations on occupiers of property and their business, often have an impact in dilapidations claims.

That they do is because most leases contain provisions requiring the tenant to comply with statutes and regulations that, apparently, affect the property.

Careful consideration needs to be given to the particular statute, regulation or by-law. Some operate if certain notice is given so, if no notice has been given, then the covenant does not bite. Some do not affect property in existence at the time the legislation is introduced, so older properties will be excluded from their ambit.

Examples of legislation that are regularly considered are: the *Health and Safety at Work etc. Act 1974*, the *Disability Discrimination Act 1995* and the *Control of Asbestos at Work Regulations 2002*.

In the case of asbestos, for example, although known to be harmful, the fact that it is present in a property does not necessarily mean that there is an obligation to remove it. While the asbestos remains 'in repair' or undisturbed, no such obligation arises (although it might as a result of legislation like the *Health and Safety at Work etc. Act 1974*). But if asbestos affected parts of the property fall into disrepair or if an area of the property is out of repair and can only be repaired in a manner that, somehow, would cause the asbestos to be disturbed, then, at the very least, the asbestos affected area would have to be isolated or, more likely, removed. In such circumstances, the work to the asbestos related area should be undertaken in accordance with the relevant guidelines. Equally, if the tenant installed the asbestos contrary to relevant legislation and therefore (in all likelihood) in breach of the lease, the landlord could look to the tenant for the cost of removal. (Surveyors should consult the RICS guidance note, *Asbestos and its implications for members and their clients*, published in 2003).

In the case of other types of legislation, e.g. the *Health and Safety at Work etc. Act* or the *Disability Discrimination Act* (the DDA), and dilapidations claims at the end of the lease, arguably there is limited impact, because the provisions depend on the presence of a workplace or provision of services to the public – in neither case would that be the case if the lease has come to an end and the tenant has vacated. During the course of the lease, the position might be different and the legislation may have to be implemented simply to comply with the terms of the lease. But more often than not, the decision as to how the legislation is satisfied will be one for the tenant, not the landlord.

Further in the case of the *Health and Safety at Work etc. Act*, it is sometimes asserted that the effect of it is to require the introduction of modern lighting that is intended, for example, to reduce eyestrain. But one should note that while certain types of expensive or complicated lighting designs are employed, for the purposes of compliance with the lease and *Landlord and Tenant* law, there will often be alternative solutions to give effect to the legislative requirements. They may be cheaper than removing expensive equipment and might be all that the landlord can insist upon. In other words, the existence of the legislation will not necessarily inevitably result in expensive works being carried out.

One would have thought that similar principles would apply to the DDA. In addition, one might imagine that, since the obligations primarily affect the public service provider or an employer, in the case of a letting of the whole of the property, it will be the tenant who has the obligation to comply with the DDA and, in the case of multi-let property, it might be the landlord. Again, there may be a variety of ways in which the DDA can be satisfied and, in a dilapidations case, it will not necessarily be for the landlord to dictate which option should be (or should have been) implemented.

2.9 TO COMPLY WITH HEAD LEASE

Where there is a subtenancy, it is often the case that the sublease will require the subtenant to comply with the majority of the obligations of the head tenancy (the covenant to pay the head rent is usually excepted and often the covenant is limited to those parts of the property which are the subject of the subtenancy) or the head tenant covenants to comply with the terms of the head tenancy (either in full or in so far as they are not within the obligations of the subtenant).

Of course, as with the principal terms of any lease, one will have to understand the inter-relationship between the terms of the head lease and the sublease and the extent to which they set out a consistent and complete code for the maintenance of the property. That may not always be readily achievable with there being doubt about the extent of the liability of one or the other. Further, there may be issues about the entitlement, during the continuance of the head lease, of the head landlord to take enforcement action against the subtenant and vice versa, with the *Landlord and Tenant (Covenants) Act* 1995 also having an impact. If the position is unclear in these respects, specific legal advice will be required.

Further, notwithstanding that the terms of the relevant provisions of the leases are identical, it will not always follow that the subtenant will, in practice (or as a matter of law) have the same obligations as the head tenant. As will be seen in Chapter 5, *The work required and its extent*, the extent of a tenant's obligations can be influenced by, for example, the duration of the tenancy – the shorter the term, the less likely it is that it would have been contemplated that the subtenant would be responsible for the undertaking of major and costly works.

Walker v Hatton (1842)

Just this point was illustrated in a case where the sublease was granted just over two years after the head lease was entered into and was for a period equivalent to the head lease less ten days. The court held that the subtenant's covenants were not the same as those of the head tenant notwithstanding the similarity between the wording of the relevant clauses in each lease.

Once the head lease comes to an end, the landlord will become the direct landlord of the subtenant but whether the relationship will be governed by the terms of the expired head lease or the sublease will depend on the manner by which the head lease came to an end. If the head lease simply expires and the subtenant remains in possession by virtue of, say, an entitlement under the security of tenure provisions of Part II of the *Landlord and Tenant Act* 1954, then until a new lease is granted (or ordered by the court, if terms have not been agreed and the appropriate court application has had to be made), the subtenant will hold the property under the terms of the sublease. However, if the head lease is surrendered, the relationship will be governed by the terms of the head lease by virtue of section 139 of the *Law of Property Act* 1925. If the head lease has become forfeit, then the sublease would also have come to an end. While the subtenant could seek reinstatement of its tenancy (by way of relief from forfeiture), it is possible that, as a condition for having its tenancy reinstated, the court could require the subtenant to take a lease in terms that incorporate some or all of the terms of the forfeit head lease, or that the subtenant makes good the breach of covenant committed by the former head tenant which could then result in the subtenant carrying out works of repair that should have been undertaken by the head tenant.

2.10 PLANT/MACHINERY/SERVICES

It would be a rare property intended to be let that would be without plant, machinery or services; it will require electricity, plumbing, heating and may require security equipment. In other words, a property needs more than four walls and a roof – it needs the things that make it 'work'.

Therefore, in almost all dilapidations claims one will need to understand the approach intended to be adopted by the landlord and tenant in respect of such services and the steps required to be taken to comply with the lease obligations as they concern such services.

One approaches a dilapidations claim in respect of services in generally the same way one considers the covenants as to the form and condition of the property. How does the lease deal with such matters? Does it cover services at all or just limit obligations to, say, the structure?

But, there are some aspects of services that will result in some variation of approach. Primarily this is due to the difference in life expectancy between a property and services. A property may be expected to last for very many years longer than some services which will, inevitably, fall more quickly into disrepair with age and the more intensive, regular, use to which they are put.

In addition, differences are frequently encountered in the drafting of covenants as they affect services. So, for example, covenants might require the services to be kept in good condition, or they may require the maintenance of the services, or the services to be kept in good working order. In such cases, it may well be that, particularly when linked with more usual repairing obligations, wording like this will result in more being required to be done to ensure the covenant is satisfied.

Ultraworth Ltd v General Accident Fire & Life Assurance Corp plc (2000)

It is sometimes contended that, because a certain period of time has passed or is soon to pass, the services require replacement or renewal. While one might do that by choice, in dilapidations claims such an approach would be incorrect. What matters is whether the services concerned are functioning and that the covenants that affect them have been satisfied. For example, as in this case, one might want to install modern, more efficient, air-conditioning equipment, but if the equipment in place is in repair and functioning properly, there is unlikely to be any breach of the lease.

Fluor Daniel Properties Ltd v Shortlands Investments Ltd (2001)

Commenting on the use of guidelines as to the life expectancy of services in a case concerning service charges, the judge said:

> 'I therefore reject the notion that merely because an item of plant has reached the end of its recommended lifespan, as suggested by the [Chartered Institution of Building Services Engineers] or some other guidelines, it was, and is reasonable for Shortlands to want to replace it at the tenants' expense.'

Mason v Totalfinaelf UK Ltd (2003)

In a case concerning a petrol station where the judge concluded that a means of testing whether the fuels tanks were leaking had not been followed fully so that evidence about the process was of little help, he said:

> 'Given the failure fully to carry through the MTCF methodology, the notion that they were not [in good and substantial condition] is founded simply upon their age at that date coupled with an appeal to the indisputable view that there is likely to come a time when the tanks will fail, although quite when nobody can say. In my judgment, that is insufficient to establish a breach of clause 3(4).'

Although the problem of deciding whether an item should be replaced or repaired bit by bit concerns property generally, it is of particular concern with services. Provided what is proposed is what a reasonable surveyor would recommend and that there is some disrepair to the services (or parts of them), it is likely that, notwithstanding the fact that work will be done to parts of the services that are not, at that time out of repair, it will still be work of repair.

Further, by the time most types of services fall out of repair, manufacturing methods or governing regulations have moved on and it is frequently either impossible or disproportionately expensive to either repair the existing item or to replace with the same product. Inevitably, therefore, it is frequently the case that there will be arguments about the improvement that flows from the introduction of modern replacements for services in disrepair or from compliance with current regulations. Provided what is proposed is what a reasonable surveyor would recommend, it is likely that, notwithstanding the inevitable improvements that flow from the work, it will still be work of repair.

Morcom v Campbell-Johnson (1956)

Although not a case directly concerning dilapidations, but nonetheless considering works in respect of which the court had to decide whether they were improvements or repairs, it was held that:

> 'If the work which is done is the provision of something new for the benefit of the occupier, that is, properly speaking, an improvement; but if it is only the replacement of something already there, which has become dilapidated or worn out, then, albeit that it is a replacement by its modern equivalent, it comes within the category of repairs and not improvements.'

2.11 BREAK OR RENEWAL CLAUSES

Although not setting out obligations in the sense of the covenants considered so far, many leases contain provisions allowing for one party or both to bring the lease to an end before the expiry of the contractual term. Some leases also allow a tenant to renew a lease. In either case, such clauses often require compliance to greater or lesser extent with the terms of the lease if the clause is to be validly operated by the tenant. Whether compliance is judged at the date of the giving of the (usually) requisite notice or at the date the notice takes effect depends on an analysis of the terms of the lease. Further, there can be debate on the degree of compliance required – in some cases full compliance is required, in others reasonable compliance and in others substantial compliance.

In addition to arguments about whether the conditions for an effective break have been satisfied, an all too frequently encountered problem is ensuring the validity of the break notice itself. There have been a raft of cases on the issue. Most notable was *Mannai Investment Co Ltd v Eagle Star Life Assurance Co Ltd* which makes it clear that a notice must strictly comply with any specific contractual requirements as to its form or contents but that, in other respects, all that is now required is that a break notice leaves a reasonable recipient in no doubt that the right is being exercised and how and when the notice will operate. Nonetheless, problems continue to arise and landlords continue to seek to exploit them if it means the prospect of keeping the tenant 'on the hook'.

Peer Freeholds Ltd v Clean Wash International Ltd (2005)

In this case the notice (as in *Mannai*) specified an incorrect break date. The court held that the intention of the notice that was given was clear, that there was a mere mistake as to the break date specified and therefore the notice was valid.

Grainger Trust plc v Micros-Fidelio UK Ltd (2003)

This case emphasised the importance of full compliance with the terms of a break clause. The lease provided that 'if the tenant has complied with all his obligations in this lease down to the date of termination of the lease then in either case the term shall cease on that date'. A schedule of dilapidations was served by the landlord on the tenant and the tenant also owed over £3,500 in rent arrears. The tenant purported to exercise the break clause in the lease. It was held that the inclusion of the words 'in either case' was of no benefit to the clause and was meaningless. Those words could be safely disregarded, leaving the clause as a standard form of break clause. There was no evidence to show that the tenant had attempted to comply with its obligations or that it had made any attempt to remedy its breaches. The court was satisfied, having regard to photographs of the property and the alleged breaches, that the tenant's purported exercise of the break clause was ineffective. On a true construction of the clause and taking into account subsequent events, the tenant's purported exercise of the break clause was ineffective and the lease remained extant.

Fitzroy House Epworth Street (No. 1) Ltd and another v The Financial Times Ltd (2005)

The lease contained a break clause allowing the defendant to terminate on notice, as long as it had materially complied with all its obligations under the lease. The tenant served a termination notice seeking to break the lease. It undertook substantial works of renovation and repair to ensure that it had fully complied with the repairing covenants. It then purported to terminate by vacating the premises on the termination date. The landlords contended that the tenant was in breach of its lease, in that the property remained in disrepair, so that the lease had not been successfully terminated. The landlords contended, among other things, that the 'material compliance' condition meant that the only permitted breaches as at the break date would be trivial matters, such as a missing screw or similar. The landlords' claim was dismissed. The lease had been terminated. Any breaches were either minor or trivial and the overall damage to the reversion was negligible or nil. Not every defect had to be remedied. The obligation was to put and keep in substantial repair. This did not include minor defects. The standard of repair was that to be expected by the reasonably minded tenant coming into the lease. Regard should be had to the age, type, location and established use of the building at that date, and the choice of repair methods would be left to the tenant, where applicable. The obligation was continuing and comprised both undertaking the work and achieving an acceptable outcome. A breach was material only if, in all the circumstances, and having regard to the proper efforts of the tenant to comply with its covenants and to the adverse effects on the landlord of any failure to do so, it would be fair and reasonable to refuse the tenant the privilege otherwise granted by the lease. The purpose of limiting the right to exercise a break clause was to enable a landlord to preserve its legitimate interest in ensuring compliance with all a tenant's covenants before it departed. A breach of a repairing covenant would be material only if it jeopardised the interests of the landlord so as to prevent it re-letting speedily, maintaining the value of its reversion and preserving its income stream by way of further rent.

John Laing Construction Ltd v Amber Pass Ltd (2004)

The claimant tenant held a lease from the defendant landlord. The lease contained a break clause that provided that, upon the payment of the equivalent of 12 months' rent and 'upon yielding up of the entirety of the demised premises' at the expiry of the notice, the term would cease and determine. The tenant gave notice. Although the tenant had vacated the property by that date, it had left in place a number of security barriers and security guards because of a continuing and serious problem of vandalism and trespass. The landlord contended that, by reason of the security barriers, the presence of the security guards and the failure to offer up the keys, the tenant had not formally yielded up the property, and the lease therefore continued. The court held that the lease had determined: there was no prescribed form or procedure for 'yielding up'. In the case of a unilateral termination of a lease, the task of the court was to look objectively at what had occurred and to determine whether:

- a clear intention had been manifested by the party seeking a termination to effect such termination; and
- the landlord could, if it so wanted, occupy the property without difficulty or objection.

Retention of the keys did not signify an intention by the tenant to assert any rights in respect of the property. The continued presence of security staff and the barriers did not create any hindrance to the landlord. The tenant had plainly and obviously manifested a desire to terminate the lease.

Where such clauses do impose conditions if they are to be validly operated, it can sometimes be very difficult if not impossible to achieve compliance. If that is a risk, the tenant may have no option but to seek to negotiate with the landlord the release of the conditions, often by an early settlement of any dilapidations claim. But such an approach is merely practical – there can be no guarantee that, without actual compliance with the lease, the clause will have been satisfied.

2.12 COSTS AND FEES

Although the interpretation and enforcement of many lease provisions can be expensive, the costs incurred in a dilapidations claim can be disproportionately high when considering the 'value' of the disrepair and the available remedies.

So, the ability to recover the costs and fees incurred in such cases will be an important consideration when deciding what, if any, action the landlord or tenant might take when pursuing a claim.

Many modern leases make comprehensive provision for the recovery of costs and fees; older leases perhaps less so. Of course, such provisions are inevitably going to provide for payments to the landlord. Although not impossible, it would be very unusual to find a lease that made express provision for the payment of costs and fees to the tenant.

Although it is probably fair to say that many dilapidations claims are resolved without recourse to litigation, even a settlement is unlikely to be achieved without fees having been incurred.

2.12.1   Pre-litigation costs and fees

Of course, a claim does not arise unless there has been some breach of the terms of the tenancy. That means that someone will have to inspect the property to ensure that the covenants have been met. It is only once such an inspection has taken place that one can know whether or not they have been met. In reality, such an inspection will generally be carried out by a surveyor.

The question arises, therefore, whether or not the fees incurred in considering the tenant's compliance with the terms of the lease can be recovered. In a comprehensively drafted lease, there may be provision for the recovery of such costs. In the absence of such a clause, it would seem that such 'investigative' costs cannot be recovered.

Lloyds Bank Ltd v Lake (1961)

In a case concerning, among other things, the recoverability of the solicitors' and the surveyor's costs, the judge said:

> 'In a strictly drawn lease there is often found a specific provision making the lessee liable for such expenses … In this state of the authorities and of the practice, as I know it, I must follow the decision in *Maud v Sandars*, and if a different practice is to be laid down, this must be by the Court of Appeal. For these reasons I must disallow the claim to include in the plaintiffs' damages their own solicitors' and surveyor's charges in respect of the schedule on the defendant's lease. The plaintiffs are entitled to recover the sum of £715.'

As a result of the general principle that such costs are not recoverable, most leases make provision for recovery. Obviously, the precise form of wording in each case will have to be scrutinised to understand the range of heads of the costs and fees that could be recovered.

Many leases allow for the costs of the preparation and service of a notice under section 146 of the *Law of Property Act* 1925 (the preliminary notice required for all non-rent breaches of covenant where the landlord elects to forfeit the lease – see Chapter 6, *Remedies*). But that does not necessarily cover work ancillary to the preparation and service of such a notice or work that follows the service of the notice. However, some clauses do not limit the costs recovery to the preparation and service of a section 146 notice, but also allow for costs incurred in contemplation of action under section 146. That would assist in the more complete costs recovery, but only in the context of forfeiture proceedings.

Where the landlord wishes to implement some other remedy available to it, there will need to be a more comprehensive costs clause to enable it to pursue recovery against the tenant. The most modern of clauses seek to cover every possible situation, whether before or after the expiry of the lease.

Notwithstanding that, there is still often scope for argument about costs incurred in some aspects of a dilapidations claim, e.g. negotiations before proceedings commence or participation in a mediation. Such activities are encouraged by the *Civil Procedure Rules* (the rules by which civil, as opposed to criminal, disputes are governed), yet unless a lease makes express provision for them, it would be rare to be able to recover them. However, since the continuation of a dispute (particularly a dilapidations claim) could result in significant expense, notably for the tenant, notwithstanding the likely absence of an obligation to pay such costs, a proposal might be made in relation to them if it could bring about a settlement. That said, if an offer is to be made in respect of costs that are not obviously recoverable, it should be made clear why the offer is to be made. Indeed, it may be that an offer should be made under rule 36 (Part 36) of the *Civil Procedure Rules* (see below) because, if the dispute continues and the recipient of such an offer fails to better it in court, that person may be exposed to harsher costs orders than might otherwise have been made.

2.12.2 Litigation costs and fees

If, however, the dispute cannot be resolved, then it may be appropriate for the claim to become the subject of litigation. While significant costs might have been incurred already, possibly as a result of compliance with the Protocol (which can involve the production of valuations under section 18 of the *Landlord and Tenant Act* 1927), if court proceedings are initiated, the costs will escalate. It might frequently be the case that, as a result of the rigours of dilapidations litigation, a number of professionals will be required to provide reports and attend the trial to give evidence. Such professionals include building surveyors, valuation surveyors, and mechanical and electrical experts, in addition to the team of lawyers and their client. With the acceleration in the increase in costs, the possibility of costs recovery takes on a greater importance.

Under Part 43 of the *Civil Procedure Rules*, if the court decides to make an order about costs, the general rule is that the unsuccessful party will be ordered to pay the costs of the successful party; but the court may make a different order. In deciding what order (if any) to make about costs, the court must have regard to all the circumstances of the case, including:

(a)   the conduct of all the parties;

(b)   whether a party has succeeded on part of his case, even if he has not been wholly successful; and

(c)   any payment into court or admissible offer to settle made by a party which is drawn to the court's attention (whether or not made in accordance with Part 36).

When considering the conduct of the parties, the court will examine:

(a)   conduct before, as well as during, the proceedings and in particular the extent to which the parties followed any relevant pre-action protocol (which, given its widespread use by the property industry and inclusion in the Guidance Note, should include the Protocol);

(b)   whether it was reasonable for a party to raise, pursue or contest a particular allegation or issue;

(c)   the manner in which a party has pursued or defended his case or a particular allegation or issue; and

(d)   whether a claimant who has succeeded in his claim, in whole or in part, exaggerated his claim.

Part 36 of the *Civil Procedure Rules* sets out the procedures to be followed when litigants (or potential litigants) wish to try and settle a dispute in a manner that could afford them some protection in respect of either the costs of the litigation generally or in relation to the costs still to be incurred. If a litigant makes a Part 36 offer to settle or payment and it is not accepted, the case proceeds to trial and the offeror succeeds by beating the Part 36 offer made, then, bearing in mind the court's general powers in relation to costs summarised above, not only would the offeror expect to receive the benefit of an order for costs against the other party, but the court might further penalise the other side by making them pay a higher proportion of cost or by paying interest at a higher rate. Given the potential impact of an offer to settle or payment, the well-advised party to a dispute should obtain specialist legal advice when formulating and making the offer.

When the court comes to make its decision on what costs orders to make, it has a pretty free hand. It can make an order that a party must pay:

(a)   a proportion of another party's costs;

(b)   a stated amount in respect of another party's costs;

(c)   costs from or until a certain date only;

(d)   costs incurred before proceedings have begun;

(e)   costs relating to particular steps taken in the proceedings;

(f)   costs relating only to a distinct part of the proceedings; and

(g)   interest on costs from or until a certain date, including a date before judgment.

Johnsey Estates (1990) Ltd v Secretary of State for the Environment, Transport and the Regions (2001)

In this case that concerned dilapidations and bearing in mind the principles concerning costs, the court made orders for costs based on the issues in dispute and which party had been successful in particular respects.

As a result, it can often be the case that, in addition to the other considerations that come into play when the amount of costs claimed are assessed by the court and which can suppress the sums that might be recovered, even a 'winning' litigant will not be entitled to recover all of the costs to which it would otherwise be entitled.

One should bear in mind that it is extremely rare for a litigant to recover all the costs it incurs – for reasons beyond the remit of this book, there is almost always a shortfall between the costs incurred in pursuing a claim and the costs that can be recovered even if the litigant is wholly successful in its claim. There is no hard and fast rule on the subject, but that shortfall can often be in the region of 25 per cent and sometimes as much as 50 per cent of the costs incurred.

When one adds in consideration of the factors outlined above to which the court can have regard when considering what costs orders to make, one can readily see that there are clear incentives to try and avoid the uncertainty of litigation outcome just on the question of costs, let alone the substantive dilapidations claim at the heart of the dispute. All too easily one can pursue a claim incurring all the costs involved only to recover sums that in fact leave a 'winning' litigant out of pocket. In other words, one would suggest that there has to be a clear commercial case for pursuing a dilapidations claim through litigation if one is going to embark on such activity.

There are, of course, many other issues to consider in the context of litigation, but they are outside the scope of this section and of the book more generally.

3
Limitations on 'dilapidations' covenants and claims

While many modern leases contain extensive provisions intended to define, to the smallest detail, the relationship of landlord and tenant, as has been seen that is not always the case. Sometimes leases are not as complete as one might have hoped or there is no written lease at all.

Many modern leases are favourable to the landlord. However, sometimes as a result of negotiation before the lease is entered into, some leases contain what are intended to be provisions more favourable to the tenant.

In such cases, or cases where the lease terms are implied or not as complete as one would have hoped, there may be, either expressly or impliedly, provisions the effect of which is to limit the liability of the landlord or tenant as regards the form and condition of the property.

Moreover, there are other principles of law that apply no matter what the express or implied terms of the lease.

This chapter seeks to consider how the covenants as to the form and condition of the property are sometimes limited or how claims could sometimes be prevented or prohibited. They are not considered in any particular order.

3.1 LIMITATION PERIOD

It is well known that by virtue of the *Limitation Act* 1980 a claimant's ability to enforce an obligation or make a claim is time limited in many cases. A claim for arrears of rent, for example, must be made within six years of when it fell due otherwise the entitlement to pursue it will be lost. If a claim is initiated beyond the passing of the limitation period, it will generally fail. There are exceptions, but it is beyond the scope of this book to consider them.

Limitation Act 1980, section 8

Leases are often entered into under seal or are entered into as a deed. As such they are what is known as a 'specialty'. In the case of a breach of the terms of a specialty, the limitation period is 12 years from the date of the breach (except for non-payment of rent, when it is 6 years).

It should be remembered however that in the case of a breach of the repairing obligations in a lease, it is generally the case that a new breach occurs every day the property remains out of repair.

Limitation Act 1980, section 5

In the case of leases not entered into under seal or as a deed (for example, tenancies created by implication and many short-term residential tenancies) but are simple contracts, the limitation period is six years from the date of the breach.

3.2 DURATION OF COVENANT

There are a number of factors that can work to limit the duration of a party's obligations under a lease. Of impact are express lease terms and the *Landlord and Tenant (Covenants) Act* 1995 (previously considered under 1.8, 'The parties and dilapidations claims'). The 1995 Act came into force on 1 January 1996.

3.2.1 Tenancies entered into before the commencement of the 1995 Act

(a) Original landlord and tenant

The original landlord and tenant would remain liable under the terms of the lease until its contractual expiry (unless there is some contractual provision to other effect, e.g. by limiting liability to the period that the relevant interest remains vested in the landlord or tenant).

(b) Assignee of the landlord and/or tenant's interest

An assignee of the landlord and/or tenant's interest will remain liable under the covenants of the lease for so long as the reversion or the term granted by the lease remains vested in the assignee. Further, liability only arises in respect of breaches during the period of ownership of the relevant interest.

The rights they have differ slightly. In the case of an assignee of the landlord's reversionary interest, by virtue of section 141 of the *Law of Property Act* 1925, the new landlord can enforce breaches of covenant by the tenant during the period of 'ownership' of the preceding landlord.

Smith v Muscat (2003)

The tenant may, however, be able to set off claims against the former landlord in defence of a claim made by virtue of section 141 by an assignee of the landlord.

However, assignees of the tenant's interest cannot act on breaches of covenant by the landlord before the assignee became the tenant, although its predecessor can.

Edlington Properties Ltd v JH Fenner & Co Ltd (2005)

Where a freeholder had agreed to build a factory and a party had agreed to take a lease of that factory, and after the lease had begun the freeholder had assigned the reversion to an assignee, the lessee was not entitled to set off a claim for damages against the original freeholder, for defective construction of the building, against post-assignment rent due to the assignee.

(c) Assignee of landlord and/or tenant who has given a covenant

It often happens that, on an assignment of the term granted by the lease, the incoming tenant enters into a direct covenant with the landlord to comply with the terms of the lease. In such a case it would remain liable under the terms of the lease until its contractual expiry (unless there is some contractual provision to other effect, e.g. by limiting liability to the period that the relevant interest remains vested in the incoming tenant).

(d) Landlord and/or tenant in whom the reversion or the term is vested at the end of the contractual term where there is a statutory continuation of the lease

Where the lease continues beyond its contractual expiry date by virtue of some statutory intervention (for example, Part II of the *Landlord and Tenant Act* 1954 which gives security of tenure to qualifying business tenants), the obligations will continue also for the landlord and/or tenant in whom the reversion or the term is vested at the end of the contractual term. The position could be different in respect of covenants that relate to the expiry of the term (e.g. to yield up), but one would have thought that such covenants would be deemed to 'bite' when the continued tenancy actually comes to an end.

(e) Guarantors

A guarantor will remain liable for the duration of the guarantee. To establish that, one must consider the terms of the guarantee. A guarantee is only effective if it is in writing (by virtue of the *Statute of Frauds* 1677) and, therefore, there should always be a document to consider; it will never be a question of considering what the terms might be of some implied guarantee.

Many guarantees are given on the basis that they are limited to the performance of the obligations of a particular tenant and, further, for only so long as that party remains tenant. So, for example, the guarantee of an original tenant's obligations may have come to an end on the assignment of the lease to another while the obligations of the original tenant will continue – see (a) above. Further, most guarantees come to an end if the liability of the tenant whose compliance with the lease has been guaranteed itself comes to an end.

Hindcastle Ltd v Barbara Attenborough Associates Ltd (1997)

The insolvency of the tenant, as illustrated in this case, will not release the guarantor if the lease is disclaimed by the liquidator of a company tenant or the trustee in bankruptcy of an individual tenant.

3.2.2 Tenancies entered into after the commencement of the 1995 Act

(a) Original tenant

The original tenant remains liable under its covenants for so long as the tenancy remains vested in it. On assignment, however, it is released from its covenants (as tenant and for the future) and no longer has the benefit of the landlord's covenants. But, if assignment requires permission and it is not obtained, there will be no release.

(b) Assignee of tenant (whether or not a covenant is given)

An assignee of the lease will be liable under the covenants of the lease for so long as the lease remains vested in the assignee. The assignee too is released from its covenants (as tenant and for the future) on any further assignment. But, if assignment requires permission and it is not obtained, there will be no release.

(c) Original tenant or assignee who has been required to enter into an authorised guarantee agreement

As noted above, on an assignment of the lease, the original tenant or assignee will be released from the tenant's covenants. The exception to that is when the tenant (from time to time) is contractually obliged on any assignment to enter into an authorised guarantee agreement (as provided for by section 16 of the *Landlord and Tenant (Covenants) Act* 1995). The effect of an authorised guarantee agreement is that the outgoing tenant becomes the guarantor of the performance of the tenant's covenants by its assignee. But it applies only to its assignee – once there is a further assignment, the obligations of the earlier tenant come to an end entirely. However, the assignee who is then transferring the lease may itself be required to enter into an authorised guarantee agreement and so the position continues.

(d) Original landlord

The original landlord under the lease is liable under the terms of the lease until its contractual expiry. The 1995 Act does not allow for an automatic release of the landlord from its obligations on an assignment of the reversionary interest.

However, the 1995 Act does establish a procedure by which a landlord can seek a release by the service of a notice and, if necessary, an application to the County Court.

(e) Assignee of the landlord

The effect of the 1995 Act is that the new landlord becomes subject to the burden of any covenants that bound the predecessor. The assignee landlord also takes the benefit of the tenant covenants, but not in respect of any period prior to the assignment to the new landlord (this should be contrasted with the position in respect of tenancies entered into prior to the 1995 Act coming into force as to which section 141 of the *Law of Property Act* 1925 applied). It is not entirely clear, but it seems possible that the effect of the 1995 Act is to make an assignee of the landlord liable for the landlord covenants throughout the remainder of the lease; it is not clear that the release provisions mentioned in the preceding section apply to assignees of the reversion – if they do apply, then it would seem that such assignees are in a worse position than they were prior to the 1995 Act, being then liable only during the period that the reversion was vested in the assignee landlord.

(f) Guarantors

The position of guarantors to tenancies entered into after the 1995 Act came into force is largely the same as those entered into before that date (see above). As a gloss on that position, however, if the effect of the 1995 Act is to release a tenant from liability on assignment, the guarantor will be similarly released. But, note the position where an assignment is entered into unlawfully (see (a) and (b) above).

3.3 INSOLVENCY OF TENANT OR GUARANTOR

The insolvency of a tenant or a guarantor can have the effect of, at least, crystallising liability. It can also have the effect of bringing to an end the liabilities of the tenant (by disclaimer) or can prevent enforcement action being taken without the permission of the court having first been obtained.

A detailed examination of the various different types of insolvency and the impact on the entitlement of a landlord to enforce the terms of a lease or a guarantee is outside the scope of this book.

Specific legal advice should be sought. Where it is sought, the lawyer will want to know what type of insolvency procedure has come about (liquidation, bankruptcy, administration, etc.) and when and what notices (if any) have been served.

Some types of insolvency procedure have the effect of preventing a landlord from fully enforcing the terms of the lease without first having obtained the court's permission. Whether and how the permission will be given will itself depend on the type of insolvency procedure in place and the extent to which, for example, the procedure is designed to allow the tenant or guarantor to trade its way out of trouble or whether it is just intended to bring to an end in an orderly manner the business of the tenant or guarantor.

In the case of two types of insolvency (liquidation for a company or bankruptcy for an individual), in limited cases, the lease can be brought to an end by the liquidator or the trustee in bankruptcy. The process requires the giving of a notice disclaiming the lease (i.e. putting the lease out of the 'estate' of the insolvent tenant).

Where a lease is disclaimed and it is still vested in the original tenant, it will come to an end. If the lease has been vested in an assignee (which is the tenant that has become subject to such a regime), the lease will not come to an end unless the landlord acts in a manner inconsistent with its continuance. But if the landlord does not act in such a manner, the lease will continue in a rather ephemeral way with those not released from its covenants still liable even though they may not have possession or control of the property.

Hindcastle Ltd v Barbara Attenborough Associates Ltd (1997)

The insolvency of the tenant will not release the guarantor if the lease is disclaimed by the liquidator of a company tenant or the trustee in bankruptcy of an individual tenant.

3.4 CONTRACTUAL LIMITATIONS

A lease may contain provisions the effect of which is to limit the scope or operability of the obligations as to the form and condition of the property. Obviously, there could be many ways by which a landlord and tenant might agree that the obligations of one or both of them might be limited. This section will consider some of the more frequently encountered.

3.4.1 Limited or no covenant

Issues concerning the nature and extent of the frequently encountered covenants concerning the form and condition of the property were considered above.

However, it is worth remembering the covenant itself may limit the extent of the landlord's or tenant's (or both) obligations.

By way of obvious example, unless there is a covenant to make or carry out improvements, there is no obligation to do so. Of course, as we have seen above, it may be that improvements come about by virtue of the manner by which the covenant to repair is satisfied.

Moreover, as was seen when considering the interpretation of the lease, there will from time to time be leases that appear not to make provision for a particular eventuality but the court determines that some obligation is implied. Further, as was also seen, there are circumstances when statute intervenes, e.g. section 11 of the *Landlord and Tenant Act* 1985 which imposes repairing obligations on landlords in short-term residential leases (see 1.6).

3.4.2 Notice of disrepair

Unless there is some limitation on the covenant, where property falls out of repair, there is an immediate duty to put it into repair. It is not the case that the landlord or tenant first has to be aware or made aware of it or that the covenantor meets the obligation if necessary work is carried out within a reasonable time.

British Telecommunications plc v Sun Life Assurance Society plc (1996)

A bulge developed in the external walls of the property concerned. These were parts of the property not demised to the tenant. The landlord covenanted to perform the obligations of the tenant in a head lease including an obligation to repair the property. The issue was whether the landlord was in breach of the repairing obligation as soon as the problem arose or only once a reasonable period of time had elapsed after its appearance. The court held that the former was the case.

The effect of the principle is that, in the case of a covenant to keep property in repair (i.e. which is to be found or implied in most modern leases), the covenantor will be obliged to take steps to ensure that disrepair does not arise in the first place because, if it does, there is an immediate breach to be remedied.

But the position is likely to be different where a landlord's obligation concerns a part of the property that is within the demise to the tenant.

British Telecommunications plc v Sun Life Assurance Society plc (1996)

In the same case discussed briefly above, the court noted that there is an exception to the general rule identified earlier (there is an immediate duty to put property into repair) where the defect occurs within an area demised. In that case, the landlord only becomes liable under its covenant when it is in possession of knowledge or information about the defect to the extent that a reasonable landlord would consider whether work was required or not but it fails to carry out necessary work with reasonable haste.

Hall v Howard (1988)

While one would expect there to be a need for actual notice, as illustrated by the court in the *British Telecommunications* case, sufficient information could be enough. In this case, the information was contained in a valuation survey prepared for the tenant that was eventually sent to the landlord for purposes other than to specifically notify it of the disrepair.

In the case of a tenant, most leases will contain a covenant to repair which is subject to the same general principle enunciated in *British Telecommunications plc v Sun Life Assurance Society plc* (i.e. there is an immediate duty to put the property into repair when it falls out of repair). However, some leases (particularly older examples) contain obligations to repair on notice. Such a covenant is to be distinguished from the variety discussed in Chapter 1; in these cases the obligation to repair (or do whatever else is required by the covenant) does not arise until the notice requirements have been met.

3.4.3 Other notice requirements

The type of notice discussed above will not necessarily involve the physical giving of a notice. Notices play a significant part in landlord and tenant law. In the context of dilapidations, notices most notably feature in the context of acquiring access to demised property or to require a tenant to reinstate alterations that it has carried out. Statutory notices also have to be given under the *Law of Property Act* 1925 and the *Leasehold Property (Repairs) Act* 1938, but they concern the enforcement of covenants once broken – see Chapter 4.

3.4.4 Access and entry to do works

Many leases contain covenants by which the tenant agrees to allow the landlord access. The most frequently encountered is that to enable the landlord to inspect and, having served a notice of disrepair on the tenant, to allow the landlord to come onto the property to carry out work that ought to have been undertaken by the tenant.

If the lease contains requirements as to the form of notice and its service (particularly the address and manner), then they must be satisfied otherwise the tenant will be free to decline access. If the landlord still enters the property, it could be trespassing or breaking the obligation to give quiet enjoyment of the property to the tenant.

So, such provisions can act as limitations on the enforceability of the lease and must be checked and satisfied.

3.4.5 Reinstatement

As discussed in 2.5, many covenants to reinstate alterations reserve to the landlord the choice as to whether or not to require the tenant to actually meet the obligation. Inevitably that means that the landlord's decision will have to be communicated to the tenant and that means the giving of notice.

Again, one should always consider the lease to identify the contractual terms as to the form of notice, its service (particularly the address and manner) and, particularly in the case of a reinstatement provision, the timing of the giving of notice.

Westminster City Council v HSBC Bank plc (2003)

As noted in 2.5.1, notice can even be given in a schedule of dilapidations rather than by the giving of some specific and separate notice.

Scottish Mutual Assurance Society Ltd v British Telecommunications plc (1994)

As was also noted in 2.5.1, the timing of giving notice could lead to difficulties for the tenant which might not by then have sufficient opportunity to carry out the necessary work.

While the courts have been reasonably flexible on that issue, what must be clear is that if the lease specifies how and when a notice to reinstate must be given, those provisions must be satisfied to ensure that the landlord does not inadvertently limit its ability to enforce the relevant covenant.

3.4.6 Access required

As has been noted under 3.4.2, 'Notice of disrepair', where a landlord has an obligation that relates to a part of the property that is demised, notice is required to be given to the landlord before the liability can arise.

It follows therefore that the tenant must give the landlord access to the demised property to enable the landlord to carry out that work.

Whereas a tenant could enforce the landlord's obligation to repair in such circumstances, it will not be able to do so if the tenant has prevented the landlord from meeting its requirements.

In other words, the tenant will have limited its ability to enforce the landlord's covenant.

Rent Act 1977, sections 3 and 148, Landlord and Tenant Act 1985, section 11(6) and Housing Act 1988, section 16

Under section 148 of the *Rent Act* 1977 and section 16 of the *Housing Act* 1988 (which both apply to residential lettings that are within the protection of those Acts), there is implied into tenancies regulated, respectively, by the *Rent Act* and the *Housing Act* a term that the tenant shall allow the landlord access to the property to carry out repairs for which the landlord has an obligation to undertake. Section 11(6) of the *Landlord and Tenant Act* 1985 requires the tenant who has the benefit of section 11 to allow access for inspection of the property, but only on 24 hours' written notice.

3.4.7 A specific state of repair and schedules of condition

It is often the case that the tenant, when taking a lease, will negotiate with the landlord that it does not have to maintain or repair the property so that it is put in a condition better than that which existed at a particular time (i.e. when the lease was entered into). That condition should be described in a schedule (which may also be photographic) and attached to the lease which will refer to it in the tenant's obligations. It is not always the case that there is such a schedule.

Without some sort of record of the condition of the property at the relevant date, it will be very difficult for the tenant to prove that it has complied with its obligations, although of course it is generally going to be the landlord who is making the claim and has the burden of proving that the relevant covenants have been broken. Using the best material available (e.g. evidence of recollection of the position and whatever documentary evidence might exist), the landlord (and the tenant) will have to piece together a description of the condition the property was then in.

Also problematic is the situation where the lease refers to a schedule of condition but none is attached to it. If the purpose of the absent schedule can be identified as being to achieve the result similar to that described in the preceding paragraph, the same steps will have to be undertaken. But, the lease may make it clear that the schedule was to define some different condition or form for the property. In such cases, while the evidence-gathering exercise to be undertaken will be largely the same, it is inevitably going to be more difficult.

Many tenants consider that to limit the obligations to repair in this manner is advantageous. However, the beneficial effect of such limitations is not always clear.

For example, the description of the condition may not always be clear enough to be of assistance to the reader, leading to a potentially costly evidence-gathering exercise.

Or, there can be serious difficulties in meeting the limited obligation to repair without actually improving the property or part of it from the condition that, contractually, it could be left in. If the property falls into disrepair greater than that described by a schedule of condition, the covenant to repair bites and work must be carried out. But, it may be impossible to reproduce the condition in which the property had been in and which is described in the schedule. For example, the schedule may show that part of a wall was decorated with paint that had started to flake. If the wall deteriorated, how does one recreate the flaking that existed at the time of the schedule? In practice, it would be impractical to achieve this either physically or economically so one might end up having the whole of the wall repainted.

Voaden v Champion and others (2002)

Although relevant to a claim in damages, if the tenant does not do what is required in a situation where the covenant is limited to a condition already out of repair, this shipping case supports the contention that a tenant would be responsible for the degree to which the item of the property concerned was in a greater state of disrepair than that, say, recorded in any schedule of condition.

It is not easy to give guidance to either a landlord or tenant in such a situation. Clearly covenants modified in this way are intended to limit the scope of the tenant's obligations and it would seem a nonsense were that not to be the effect. However, one cannot offer any more comfort than to contend that common sense should prevail. Whether it does will almost always depend on what is in issue and the amount of money at stake.

Where there is a schedule of condition that limits the extent of the repair covenant, then this will set the minimum standard of repair in which the tenant is obliged to leave a particular item. In reality, where an item has fallen into greater disrepair than is shown in the schedule of condition, it may well be that the only way to put the item into repair in accordance with the terms of the lease, as limited by the schedule of condition, is to correct the full disrepair.

In some instances (although this is a matter of fact and degree), the presence of the limitation can give rise to limits to the landlord's claim, due to the effect of diminution in value. This is because when a valuer seeks to compare the difference between a building with some disrepair (i.e. as described in the schedule of condition) and a building with more disrepair, it is often not possible to distinguish between the two.

It is worth remembering that schedules of condition are useful records of the arrangement of a building at the beginning of the term, and therefore of the extent of the landlord's fixtures and fittings. Unless the lease specifically records otherwise, where, for example, a partition or other fitting is present in the schedule, the landlord will not be able to seek its subsequent removal.

3.4.8 Conditions precedent

It is sometimes the case that, before a covenant operates, a condition has to be satisfied.

Examples of such covenants have been considered above where, for example, notice is required. In the case of obligations concerning parts of the property which are demised, notice is required before the landlord becomes liable on its covenants to repair.

But in some cases, whether or not the part of the property concerned is demised, the landlord's covenant does not take effect unless the tenant has complied with all or, more likely, some of its covenants. Such a result is frequently the aim of the draftsmen of residential long leases.

Many such leases are arranged so that the landlord carries out works or provides services the cost of which is passed on to the tenants through a service charge. In the case of property owned by a company of the tenants a service charge can be the only way of funding the cost of the landlord's obligations; such companies rarely have funds of their own (residential service charges not belonging to the landlord but being held on trust for the contributing tenants – section 42 of the *Landlord and Tenant Act* 1987).

As a consequence, attempts are made to try and limit the obligations of the landlord unless the service charge has been paid.

Yorkbrook Investments v Batten (1985)

The court concluded that the landlord's obligations which were said to be 'subject to the lessee paying the Maintenance Contribution' did not create a condition precedent. The court contended that if the clause operated in the manner suggested by the landlord, none of the services to be provided would need to be even if there was an innocent explanation for the failure to pay the service charges.

Bluestorm Ltd v Portvale Holdings Ltd (2004)

In a lease with a provision apparently intended to reach the same result, the court said that, had it been required to make a decision on the issue (which it was not), it would have concluded that there was a condition precedent which would have meant that the *Yorkbrook* decision would have been overruled. Since the court did not have to actually decide the point, *Yorkbrook* remains current (but doubted) case law.

3.5 ESTOPPEL

Where a landlord conducts itself in a way relied on by the tenant, it could be the case that, notwithstanding options the landlord could otherwise have taken, it could be prevented from subsequently doing so (i.e. it is estopped from doing so). Such a concept is known as 'estoppel'. It can apply to many situations.

There are two obvious ways in which the principles of estoppel might have an impact in the context of dilapidations.

Firstly, and by way of example, the landlord may be aware that the tenant has not met its repairing obligations and will not do so by the end of the lease. Knowing that the tenant is leaving so that the lease will come to an end, the landlord might tell the tenant that it does not need to carry out any work. The lease then ends and the tenant vacates losing control of the property. Relying on the landlord's 'statement' the tenant uses the money it could have applied to repairing the property for some other purpose.

If the landlord were then to attempt to enforce the covenants and claim damages for breach, the tenant could contend that the landlord was estopped from doing so. The landlord had made a representation which had been relied upon by the tenant to its detriment and it would be inequitable for the landlord to be allowed to go back on its representation.

Brikom Investments Ltd v Carr (1979)

While not directly on a dilapidations issue, the case illustrates the effect of the principle. The landlord, Brikom, offered leases of flats to the protected tenants of them. When doing so, the landlord said that it would carry out roof works at its own expense. The tenant took up the lease but, while the landlord did carry out the roof work, it sought to recover the cost of doing so from the tenant (and others) through the service charge. The court held that the landlord was estopped from doing so.

Secondly, the landlord and tenant may have agreed (specifically or by implication from their actions) that the responsibility for a part of the property lay with one or the other and then acted in reliance on that. If the circumstances warrant it, the court could conclude that it would be wrong to allow the parties to step back from the arrangement and operate their relationship in some other way.

4
Have the covenants been broken?

In practice, the most important practical dilapidations problem of all is to establish whether the covenants have been broken and, if so, to identify what work (and the extent of it) is required to correct the defect. This chapter looks at the first of these questions; the second question is considered in Chapter 5. There is a degree of overlap between the two – the standard of repair is relevant when considering whether there is in fact a breach of the lease and relevant when considering what work is required to correct a breach.

In the case of covenants, say, to decorate every five years, one can readily ascertain whether or not the covenant has been met.

Simmons v Dresden (2004)

As discussed above, it should not matter, in terms of assessing performance, whether the property needs decorating – if the covenant says one must decorate and it is not carried out, there is a breach.

In the case of the covenant to repair, unless part of the property subject to it is out of repair, the covenant has not been broken.

Quick v Taff-Ely Borough Council (1985)

In a case where the residential tenant had to endure dismal conditions as a result of condensation caused by the manner in which the windows had been constructed and the inadequate central heating system, the court was driven to conclude that, since the property had been built according to the regulations and standards of the time and the problems were not the result of damage to the part of the property that had led to their creation, there was no disrepair. (This case should be contrasted with *Welsh v Greenwich London Borough Council*, considered below, where the covenant to repair was not broken but a covenant to maintain the property in good condition was.)

Post Office v Aquarius Properties Ltd (1987)

The water table in the area in which the property was situated had risen after its construction. As a result of a defective 'kicker' joint between the walls and the floor in the basement, it became ankle deep in water. However, the joint was in exactly the same condition it had been in when the property was built. Moreover, there was no evidence that any part of the property to which the repairing covenant applied had become defective or fallen out of repair. Therefore, the court held that there was no disrepair:

> 'A state of disrepair ... connotes a deterioration from some previous physical condition.'

Lee v Leeds City Council (2002)

But, just because the item concerned is not out of repair does not necessarily mean that it will not have to be corrected. If damage has been caused to something that is within the covenant to repair, the effective performance of that covenant may mean that the design defect will have to be cured too.

Gibson Investments Ltd v Chesterton plc (No. 1) (2002)

To establish whether or not there is disrepair, a comparison needs to be made, but should that be with the property as it was at the time lease was entered into or when the property was built? In *Post Office v Aquarius Properties Ltd* the court held that the construction date was the date for comparison. The court reiterated that conclusion in this case.

But what if there is no disrepair at present? Can the covenantor carry out preventative work? Arguably a covenant to keep in repair could require such work because a landlord can be immediately liable for disrepair as soon as the property being the subject of its obligation falls out of repair (see *British Telecommunications plc v Sun Life Assurance Society plc* and *Gibson Investments Ltd v Chesterton plc* – 'The obligation to keep in repair obliges the tenant to ensure that the building does not get out of repair.').

Mason v Totalfinaelf UK Ltd (2003)

Such an argument was rejected by the court in cases where no disrepair existed.

Postel Properties Ltd v Boots the Chemist Ltd (1996)

But where part of the property that is within the covenant does fall into disrepair, then notwithstanding that some part of it is not in disrepair, replacement of the whole can amount to repair, in this case a phased replacement of the roof.

It was noted above that where the subject matter of the repairing covenant was not out of repair, notwithstanding the presence of some otherwise appalling conditions, there was no breach of the covenant. However, the position would appear, possibly, to be different if the covenant is to keep the property in good condition.

Welsh v Greenwich London Borough Council (2000)

The property suffered defects not dissimilar to those encountered in *Quick v Taff-Ely Borough Council* (see the beginning of this chapter) but in this case the covenant was to maintain the property in good condition. It was accepted that there was no disrepair to activate the covenant to repair, but the court decided that the obligation to maintain the property in good condition was different from a covenant to repair and the landlord was in breach of the covenant by not providing appropriate insulation or dry lining for the walls.

But that should not be taken as leading to the conclusion that the covenant can operate even though there has been no deterioration in condition.

Fluor Daniel Properties Ltd v Shortland Investments Ltd (2001)

The judge said:

> '... the item in question suffers from some defect (i.e. some physical damage or deterioration or, in the case of plant, some malfunctioning), such that repair, amendment or renewal is reasonably necessary. I further accept his submission that the condition of the item in question must be such as to be no longer reasonably acceptable, having regard to the age, character and locality of the premises, to a reasonably minded office tenant of the kind likely to take a lease of the property. Whether, once those conditions are established, the item must be repaired or renewed is a question of fact and degree, having regard to the nature and extent of the defect and, not least, to the costs likely to be involved.'

He concluded that there had to be some defect in the item in question, even though the terms of the covenant went beyond repair.

But even though there might be, on the face of it, disrepair, will that mean that there is a breach of covenant and that work needs to be carried out? Not always.

So, by way of simple example, assuming that there is normally a need to paint as part of the covenant to repair, the fact that some of the paintwork is flaking will not necessarily mean that remedial work must be carried out. (Of course, in that example, there may also be decoration covenant which has been broken.)

The test is set out in what is still the leading case, *Proudfoot v Hart*.

Proudfoot v Hart (1890)

> '... to keep a house in good tenantable repair the tenants' obligation is to put and keep the premises in such repair as having regard to the age, character and locality of the house, would make it reasonably fit for the occupation of a tenant of the class who would be likely to take it. The age of the house must be taken into account, because nobody

could reasonably expect that a house 200 years' old should be in the same condition of repair as a house lately built.'

Credit Suisse v Beegas Nominees Ltd (1994)

'... although *Proudfoot v Hart* ... has lost ground as to some parts of its reasoning and has been said often to have been misunderstood, the notion illustrated by it that a covenant to keep in a specified state includes an obligation to put into that state has been acted upon, by now, in probably hundreds of cases and still survives. The obligation here is thus not merely to keep in good and tenantable condition, but that the landlord should put the building into that condition.'

Mason v Totalfinaelf UK Ltd (2003)

As to standard of repair the court noted that:

'It was common ground that clause 3(4), with its reference to "well and substantially", does not require that the premises be kept in perfect repair. Equally, it was common ground that the standard to be applied should be such as, having regard to the age, character and locality of the premises at the start of the lease, would make the premises reasonably fit for a reasonably minded tenant of a class who would be likely, at that time, to take the premises, and that the appropriate standard does not alter during the term of the lease in the sense that changes in the character of the locality of the premises, or of the class of person likely to take them, do not elevate or depress what would otherwise be the standard: see, generally, *Proudfoot v Hart* (1890) and *Anstruther-Gough-Calthorpe v McOscar* (1924).'

As noted under *Gibson Investments Ltd v Chesterton plc* above, one needs to consider the date at which the comparison with the current condition of the property is made.

Anstruther-Gough-Calthorpe v McOscar (1924)

The tenant contended that one should have regard to the requirements of a reasonably minded tenant *at the end of the term of the lease*. A series of conclusions by one of the appeal judges warrant repeating:

'The tenant must when necessary restore by reparation or renewal of subsidiary parts the subject matter demised to a condition in which it is reasonably fit for the purposes for which such a subject matter would ordinarily be used. The question in dispute seems to be whether, as the purposes for which such a subject matter is ordinarily used may vary from time to time, the standard of repair is to vary from time to time, or remains as it was when the subject matter was demised ... it was a wholly untenable proposition to say that the depreciation of the neighbourhood ought to lower the amount of damages for breach of a covenant to repair ... I do not think there was any intention of suggesting that a deterioration in the class of tenants would lower the standard of repairs ... An improvement of its tenants or its neighbourhood will not increase the standard of repair, nor will their deterioration lower that standard.'

The *Proudfoot v Hart* test can be considered in its individually important constituent parts:

● the age of the property;

● the character and locality of the property; and

● the reasonably minded tenant.

4.1 THE AGE OF THE PROPERTY

Anstruther-Gough-Calthorpe v McOscar (1924)

The court considered that a consideration of the age of the property was the most important factor. An old property is not required to be made new but it can be kept in repair to protect it.

Plough Investments Ltd v Manchester City Council; Plough Investments Ltd v Eclipse Radio & Television Services Ltd (1989)

The property was built in about 1925 and was about 50 years old when the leases were granted. There was evidence that the steel frame was rusted and the landlord wanted to undertake significant work and pass on the cost to the tenants. In the course of giving judgment, the court notes that:

> 'There were cracks when the leases were granted. A building of this sort, over 60 years old, is bound, in my view, to have some cracks in the bricks or blocks.'

Pembery v Lamdin (1940)

A landlord demised an old property not constructed with a damp course or with waterproofing for the outside walls, and covenanted to keep the external part of the demised property other than the shop front in good and tenantable repair and condition. The tenant claimed that, under the covenant, the landlord was liable to waterproof the outside walls, and so render the place dry. The court held that the obligation on the landlord was only to keep the property in repair in the condition in which it was when demised, and, as it was an old property, he was not liable to do any more than point the brickwork.

4.2 THE CHARACTER AND LOCALITY OF THE PROPERTY

Proudfoot v Hart (1890)

One of the judges illustrated the issue by explaining that the repairs necessary to a palace would not be the same as those necessary for a cottage or that repairs to a house in Grosvenor Square would not be the same as those for a house in Spitalfields. (Ironically a comparison between houses in Grosvenor Square and Spitalfields, that seemed appropriate in 1890, would now probably not be made because there has been significant redevelopment in that area and while there are still differences between them, the difference is no longer so stark.)

Gibson Investments Ltd v Chesterton plc (2002)

> '"Good and substantial repair" means more than just that the building must be capable of occupation. It means, in this case, that the building must be in a state of repair that is appropriate for a high-class office building in a prime office location in Birmingham.'

4.3 THE REASONABLY MINDED TENANT

Inevitably one has to consider who or what sort of person would be a reasonably minded tenant. It will not be the actual tenant and market conditions at the time the property was let are not relevant. What is material in the context of this issue is to ascertain what would make the property fit for such a tenant's occupation. The court had to wrestle with such issues in *Mason v Totalfinaelf UK Ltd*.

Mason v Totalfinaelf UK Ltd (2003)

'... it was common ground that the standard to be applied should be such as, having regard to the age, character and locality of the premises at the start of the lease, would make the premises reasonably fit for a reasonably minded tenant of a class who would be likely, at that time, to take the premises, and that the appropriate standard does not alter during the term of the lease in the sense that changes in the character of the locality of the premises, or of the class of person likely to take them, do not elevate or depress what would otherwise be the standard ... What, however, was a matter of dispute was the assumption to be made about the nature of the class of tenant likely to take the premises at the start of the lease in 1964 ... I agree ... that the class of reasonably minded tenant likely at the commencement of the term to take the premises refers to the quality of reasonably minded tenant that would have done so, having regard to the then age, character and locality of the premises, and therefore that the standard of repair, etc. is what would make the premises reasonably fit for the occupation of such a tenant. On the face of it, since Total was the tenant that took the lease, the class of tenant was a person or organisation such as Total ... The result, in my judgment, is that the court must approach the question by asking itself, doing the best that it can, what, given the age and character of the premises (a converted inter-war dwelling-house already 30 or so years old at the time) and their locality (a semi-rural position with a fairly small road frontage, but on a trunk road leading from Crawley to East Grinstead), a reasonably minded oil company would reasonably require, at the time the lease was granted, to render the premises reasonably fit for use as a place from which to run the businesses of a petrol filling station and attached shop, together with car sales and, at the rear of the site, facilities for motor vehicle repairs.'

4.4   OTHER ISSUES CONCERNING THE STANDARD OF REPAIR

While the expected life of parts of a property can be relevant to considerations as to whether work carried out is of repair or not (it was an issue in relation to the roof of the property considered in *Postel Properties Ltd v Boots the Chemist Ltd*), the question arises whether the anticipated commercial life of the property itself is relevant to the standard of repair?

Sandhu v Ladbroke Hotels Ltd (1995)

The answer is in the negative and is explained in this case which concerned an appeal from an arbitrator on a rent review case:

'I do not find any support in authority for the "commercial life" concept ... The fact that commercial premises had been designed and built for a specialised use which had become totally obsolete (such as, for instance, Mr George's shooting gallery and fencing school between the Haymarket and Leicester Square as described in "Bleak House") would be a very strong reason for the court to decide, under the *Leasehold Property (Repairs) Act* 1938, that a tenant ought not to be held liable for substantial repairs to premises which would inevitably have to be substantially reconstructed, if not completely demolished, before long. But ... the effect of the *Leasehold Property (Repairs) Act* 1938 is not to be taken into account in determining the notional state of repair for the purposes of the rent review.'

Some tenancies (mainly short-term residential lettings) qualify the repairing obligations by directing that 'fair wear and tear is excepted'. When considering whether there is disrepair to a property subject to a lease with such a qualification, one has to understand the meaning of the expression. If a tenant uses property normally and reasonably, damage caused by such use will be excepted. If the property suffers, as it were, natural disrepair caused by the weather, the tenant will not be liable. But the damage that itself flows from damage caused by fair wear and tear will not necessarily be outwith the tenant's obligations.

Regis Property Co Ltd v Dudley (1959)

The exception for fair wear and tear in the tenant's repairing covenant did not except the tenant from responsibility for taking steps to avoid further damage deriving from a defect of repair which itself was originally due to fair wear and tear.

The result of that decision could be to reduce the effect of the 'fair wear and tear' exclusion because a tenant may be best advised to remedy the defect that would otherwise be covered by it to prevent liability arising for something that is not caught by it.

As was noted above (e.g. when considering *Welsh v Greenwich London Borough Council*), a covenant to maintain in good condition could result in the covenantor having to carry out work that would not otherwise be required by the covenant to repair. But is the approach to be adopted when considering the standard required by such a covenant any different from that required when considering the covenant to repair? Apparently not.

Credit Suisse v Beegas Nominees Ltd (1994)

Such a covenant was considered in this case and the conclusion of the court was that the standard required was akin to that defined in *Proudfoot v Hart*.

Mason v Totalfinaelf UK Ltd (2003)

But, of course, while the approach to the standard required might be similar, one must bear in mind that the effect of the 'good condition' covenant would mean that more work was required than would have been the case under a covenant to repair.

4.5 UNDEFINED WORKS

It sometimes arises that an attempt is made, usually on behalf of a landlord, to make a claim in respect of 'works' that are not obviously capable of being defined.

One cannot claim a breach where it is impossible to define what is wrong with the property; this is because it is a prerequisite of a claim for damages that there is a provable breach of an obligation. If a breach cannot be ascertained, because it is unconfirmed or not capable of definition, then it is not possible to say that any compensation is due. Thus, it is not possible to include a contingency allowance in the claim or to include provisional items, as these cannot be defined. A landlord can avoid this conundrum by actually undertaking the works itself. If, in so doing, it encounters works that were not foreseen, then these can, presuming that they are legitimate items, be added to the claim. Thus it may be a sensible tactic for the landlord to complete the works itself, so that it has a fully crystallised claim. There is little that a tenant can do to avoid this possibility once its lease has come to an end.

For the same reason, it is not appropriate to include items for the testing of equipment within the building, such as electrical testing. While some leases include an obligation to maintain the electrical system in accordance with the regulations issued by the Institute of Electrical Engineers, the testing regime is a recommendation only, rather than a prescriptive obligation. The absence of testing is not, therefore, in itself a breach of the regulations, although any disrepairs that the testing identifies could be. Thus the surveyor is faced with the choice of either identifying the nature of the disrepair or, if it is reasonable in the circumstances, completing the testing as part of the preparation of the schedule (which could result in it being at the tenant's expense, as the result of the possible existence of a covenant to pay fees).

All these matters should be borne in mind when considering whether or not the covenants as to the form and condition of the property have been satisfied. Indeed, one should have considered them and probably carried out appropriate preliminary investigations before inspecting the property for that purpose.

Reference has already been made to the Protocol and the Guidance Note. As explained in the introductory section of this book, it is not within its scope to discuss the practical steps to be taken when considering or responding to dilapidations claims – reference should be made to such publications which contain plenty of practical relevant advice on the subject.

5
The work required and its extent

Having established that there is a breach of the lease, the next step will be to consider the work required to remedy it and the extent of that work.

As mentioned in Chapter 4, there will inevitably be a degree of overlap of some of the issues considered there with those discussed now.

It is important to note immediately that it is for the covenantor to decide what course of action to adopt. Of course it might allow itself to be influenced by the action taken by the party seeking to enforce compliance, but nonetheless the choice is the covenantor's.

Gibson Investments Ltd v Chesterton plc (No. 1) (2002)

'Once it is established that there is disrepair requiring to be remedied, performance of the obligation to repair requires the covenantor to undertake such remedial work as is prudent, i.e. such methods and mode of repair as a sensible person would adopt ... the choice as to what work to carry out is that of the paying party; in this case that is agreed to be the defendant. However, the work he selects must be such as a competent, careful surveyor or other appropriate professional person would advise as being appropriate.'

Riverside Property Investments Ltd v Blackhawk Automotive (2004)

The concept was underlined that the covenantor has the freedom to choose between two appropriate solutions: repair or replacement. The case concerned asbestos cement roof sheets and the method of attaching them:

'On the evidence, the repairs carried out by the defendant had been sufficient to comply with the covenant. The continued presence of asbestos in the original roof sheets that had not been replaced could not be a reason to contend that the defendant had breached its repairing obligation. There was no evidence to suggest that the manner of carrying out the repairs was in breach of covenant. The decision to use topfix fasteners could not be criticised, and their installation by specialist roofing contractors also did not constitute a breach of covenant.'

5.1 METHOD OF REPAIR

But the 'choice' concerns methods of repair. The covenantor is not permitted to undertake work by doing something else to achieve the same purpose as the item that is out of repair.

Creska Ltd v Hammersmith & Fulham London Borough Council (1998)

The underfloor heating (embedded in concrete) was defective. The cost of the work of pure repair was going to be very high. The tenant proposed that, as an alternative to actually carrying out such work, it would install storage heaters. The landlord objected and the court agreed with it – the tenant was required to undertake the repairs. (There was a twist to the case resulting in a further decision considered under 6.2.2, 'Landlord to enter and carry out works'.)

Postel Properties Ltd v Boots the Chemist Ltd (1996)

This case illustrates a classic example of there being a choice of solutions to resolve a problem of disrepair. It concerned the roof of a shopping centre which the court accepted was within five years of the end of its predicted lifespan. Although more expensive than other options (the costs were being passed on to the tenants), for a range of reasons the court accepted that the method adopted by the landlord was within the covenant.

It must be noted, however, that in cases where the cost of the work is going to be passed on to the tenants, the landlord's choice as to the method of carrying out required work is rather more limited than if the covenantor was not entitled to pass on the cost. In particular the landlord should have regard to the length of the leases when granted.

Fluor Daniel Properties Ltd v Shortlands Investments Ltd (2001)

The standard of work to be adopted must be such as the tenants, given the length of their leases, could fairly be expected to pay for. The fact that an item of plant has reached the end of its recommended lifespan as suggested by industry guidelines does not mean that it would be reasonable for the landlord to want to replace it at the tenants' expense. The landlord was therefore not entitled to remove the air-conditioning sumps, humidifiers, cooling blocks, chillers and cooling towers and replace them with new plant, as a programme of repair was appropriate at a lower cost. Neither was it entitled to replace fan motors.

One should not forget either that even if there are alternative methods of repair, they will only be appropriate if they meet the required standard (as discussed in Chapter 4).

Proudfoot v Hart (1890)

'... to keep a house in good tenantable repair the tenants' obligation is to put and keep the premises in such repair as having regard to the age, character and locality of the house, would make it reasonably fit for the occupation of a tenant of the class who would be likely to take it.'

Whatever method is chosen, the work must remedy the defect. Work that is not required by the covenant is not permitted. So, if a landlord enters property demised to a tenant for the purpose of carrying out work intended to be repair but carries out work of pure improvement, it will probably be committing a trespass and/or breaking the covenant for quiet enjoyment. Moreover, if the landlord could otherwise recover the cost of permitted work from the tenant and others through a service charge, such costs could not be passed on.

Gibson Investments Ltd v Chesterton plc (No. 1) (2002)

As explained in the discussion of this case at 2.1.2 and 2.1.3, the person responsible for carrying out repair work should ensure that the work he carries out is not futile. In some circumstances, therefore, performance of the covenant is not achieved if the work proposed will not remedy the covenant once and for all.

Nor can or should the covenantor carry out purely preventative work.

Mason v Totalfinaelf UK Ltd (2003)

An argument in favour of purely preventative work was rejected by the court in this case where no disrepair existed.

But that can be contrasted with cases like *Postel Properties Ltd v Boots the Chemist Ltd* where an element of preventative work flowed from the work which the court concluded was within the covenant to repair.

5.2 MATERIALS AND WORKMANSHIP EMPLOYED

Just as the covenantor has the choice of method of repair where there are alternatives, it will also have a choice where there are alternatives as to materials and the workmanship employed. Which are used and employed will depend, just like the consideration of the standard of repair, on the age, character and locality of the property, and the materials and workmanship that would make it reasonably fit for the occupation of a tenant of the class who would be likely to take it.

That can give rise to problems where not all of the subject matter of the covenant is out of repair and only part needs attention. For example, one wall in a room may require redecoration but the others might not. Painting one wall will almost inevitably mean that there is a difference of finish. Should the other walls be redecorated as well? Once again the answer will depend on the standard of repair required by the covenant and the *Proudfoot v Hart* test must be considered. If one is considering a storage room in a 50-year-old warehouse on a tertiary industrial estate, the answer might be in the negative; but if one is considering brand new offices in the heart of a modern business district, the answer may be in the affirmative.

Similar issues are frequently considered in the context of modern building practice and current law. A classic example concerns asbestos. As a material it was frequently used in the construction of property. In time one became aware that it was an extremely harmful substance. But while it lies undisturbed in a property and is itself in repair, no work is required to remove it. However, if work is required to an area where asbestos is present or if the asbestos material itself falls into disrepair so that fibre and dust is released, it must be treated in accordance with current practice and regulations and the cost incurred (which will usually be greater as a consequence) will, if there are service charge provisions, usually be capable of being passed on to the tenants.

This leads on to questions about defects in property that, while not matters of disrepair themselves, can become the subject of work nonetheless. Such items are often described as inherent defects. As has been seen, not everything that might be disrepair will be required to be remedied. This is particularly the case where the work to cure a problem would amount to something different and more extensive than repair. The following cases to the end of this section consider this issue. They mainly concern the covenant to repair having its ordinary meaning and effect. Of course, there will be some covenants that are more extensive, in which case one would hope to be less concerned with understanding whether or not an item of work is required to be undertaken or not. This has been illustrated, for example, in relation to covenants to maintain property in good condition (e.g. *Credit Suisse v Beegas Nominees Ltd* and *Welsh v Greenwich London Borough Council*).

Gibson Investments Ltd v Chesterton plc (No. 1) (2002)

Where it is contended that the repair work should extend to eradicating the problem, rather than being limited to prophylactic measures, the cases establish, first, that the work will not be repair if it involves giving back to the landlord something wholly different from that which he demised, but, second, there will be circumstances in which such work can be repair even though it involves adding something to the property that was not there originally, as in *Ravenseft* and *Elmcroft*.

Ravenseft Properties Ltd v Davstone (Holdings) Ltd (1979)

The landlord took down stone cladding which had started to come away from the property and was dangerous and reinstalled it but added expansion joints that had not previously formed part of the property. The tenant contended that the expansion joints were installed to remedy what was described as an inherent defect; it was not a case that an element of the property had fallen into a worse condition than it had been in – it had been built like that. Consequently, the tenant contended that the work was not of repair and that it did not have to pay for its cost through the service charge. The court concluded that there was no concept that inherent defects could never be remedied under an obligation to repair.

Brew Bros Ltd v Snax (Ross) Ltd (1970)

Just because a lease contains a covenant to repair does not necessarily mean that all work to, apparently, restore the property to the condition it was once in would be 'repair' – it is a question of fact and degree. One must consider the particular property, the state it was in when the lease was granted, the terms of the lease, and then reach a conclusion as to whether the work said to be necessary can fairly be termed repair.

Post Office v Aquarius Properties Ltd (1987)

A covenant by a tenant to keep the demised property in good and substantial repair did not impose an obligation on the tenant to remedy a defect in the structure of the property, whether resulting from faulty design or workmanship, which had been present from the time of the construction of the property and which had caused no damage to the demised property. Since no damage to the property had been proved and the wetting of the basement floor coupled with the inconvenience caused thereby did not constitute disrepair, it followed that the tenants were under no liability to the landlords under the repairing covenant to carry out any work to the property in order to remedy the defect.

Pembery v Lamdin (1940)

A landlord demised an old property not constructed with a damp course or with waterproofing for the outside walls, and covenanted to keep the external part of the demised property other than the shop front in good and tenantable repair and condition. The tenant claimed that, under the covenant, the landlord was liable to waterproof the outside walls, and so render the place dry. The court held that the obligation on the landlord was only to keep the property in repair in the condition in which it was when demised, and, as it was an old property, he was not liable to do any more than point the brickwork.

5.3 AGE OF THE PROPERTY

The age of property is a relevant consideration when considering the standard to which it must be kept in repair (*Proudfoot v Hart*). It is also a factor when considering whether the rectification of an 'inherent defect' is within the covenant to repair. The outcome of the consideration of the cases on this point is that there is no obvious distinction between the treatment of an old property and a new one; it is just another factor to be taken into account.

Sotheby v Grundy (1947)

A lease of a newly erected house, made in 1861 for a period of 99 years, contained a covenant by the tenant to 'repair uphold support maintain' the property 'with all necessary reparations and amendments whatsoever'. In 1944 the walls were bulged, fractured and overhanging, and the house was condemned as a dangerous structure under the *London*

Building Acts and was demolished. The expenses incurred by the council were recovered from the landlord who sought to recover them from the tenant as damages for breach of the repairing covenant. The evidence showed that, contrary to the *Metropolitan Building Act* 1855, which was then in force, the main walls of the house were built entirely without, or on defective, footings and there was every likelihood that what in fact happened would happen as a result of the settling of the foundations, and that the only way in which this could have been avoided would have been by underpinning, which would have meant shoring up the property, the removal of existing foundations, stage by stage, and the substitution of a new foundation in the way of footings and concrete. The court decided that the expenses were incurred because of the inherent nature of the defect in the property, and, therefore, did not come within the terms of the repairing covenant, with the result that the landlord was not entitled to recover them from the tenant.

The judge said that the question was:

'whether it can be said that this was a building which, by its own inherent nature would, in course of time, fall into a particular condition. I am sure that that is so, but the matter does not end there, because, in view of some of the other authorities to which I have been referred, particularly *Anstruther-Gough-Calthorpe v McOscar*, it seems to me that it must be a question of degree in each case. It may be that the inherent nature of a building may result in its partial collapse. One can visualise the floor of a building collapsing, owing to defective joists having been put in ... In those circumstances, in my opinion, the damage would fall within the ambit of the covenant to repair, but, as I say, it must be a question of degree in each particular case ... That, in my view, would, in effect, be asking the tenant to give the landlord something different in kind from that which had been demised. The premises demised here were premises with insecure foundations. What the tenant would have had to do would be to put in a new foundation which would alter the nature and extent of the property demised, turning a building which, as originally constructed, would not last more than some 80 odd years into a building that would last for probably another 100 years.'

5.4 CONDITION OF THE PROPERTY WHEN LET

While the *Proudfoot v Hart* test requires a consideration, among other things, of the age of the property leading to a comparison between its current state and the nature of it when built, when considering the question of the remedying of defects that go beyond pure repair and whether they fall within the covenant to repair nonetheless, a further factor is the condition of the property when let. If the property was in a good condition when let, that might be an indicator that the intention of the landlord and tenant was that the property should be maintained in that condition by the tenant. If, however, the problem evidencing the inherent defect is evident by the time of the letting, that might be an indicator that the landlord and tenant did not intend that the tenant should cure it.

McDougall v Easington District Council (1989)

But works which would have the effect of giving back to the landlord something different than had been let would generally be a step too far when considering whether or not they fell within the covenant to repair. An example of that would be where the works would have the effect of substantially increasing the expected life of the property and its value. In this case it had the effect of increasing the market value of the house from about £10,000 to about £18,500 and of prolonging the estimated life of the property by some 30 per cent.

5.5 LENGTH OF THE LEASE

In construing the covenant, one relevant factor is the length of the lease. The longer the lease, the more likely that the tenant will be under an obligation to remedy the defect.

Gibson Investments Ltd v Chesterton plc (No. 1) (2002)

The lease considered in this case was a relatively long term of 33 years.

Fluor Daniel Properties Ltd v Shortlands Investments Ltd (2001)

The length of term of the lease could be of even greater significance where the tenant is expected to reimburse the landlord through the service charge for works undertaken by the landlord, as in this case.

5.6 WORK BEYOND REPAIR

Of most significance to the issue as to whether work can be said to be work of repair is the nature of the work to be undertaken. The following cases consider some of the problems that arise in respect of that issue.

Lurcott v Wakely & Wheeler (1911)

The case concerned a very old house. Major work was undertaken to one wall and, in due course, it was taken down and a new, better supported wall erected. While the first element of the work did not involve complete replacement of the wall, the question as to the status of the complete replacement that came about following the second phase of the work had to be addressed:

> 'When it has got its new wall it will not be a new house; it will be the old house put into repair in the sense that there has been renewed or replaced a worn-out subordinate part of the whole.'

The case also assists in understanding the effect of modern building practice and law on the issue of remedying defects. The court concluded that it was within the covenant to rebuild according to the requirements of the county council.

However, the effect of compliance with modern building practice and law could mean that work otherwise required could be taken out of the ambit of the covenant to repair.

Pembery v Lamdin (1940)

The extent of the structural additions to the basement to make it waterproof was such that the work was held by the court to go beyond repair.

Ravenseft Properties Ltd v Davstone (Holdings) Ltd (1979)

The landlord carried out work adding expansion joints that had not previously formed part of the property. The court held that to have done so was what a sensible person (or, in this case, engineer) would have done – it was sensible building practice. (However, following what is now a familiar theme, one would contend that this result would only arise provided the work necessitated by good building practice did not of itself take the work beyond what would be repair.)

5.7 USE OF MODERN MATERIALS

It is inevitable in many cases that, when work is undertaken, more up-to-date materials and practices will be employed.

Postel Properties Ltd v Boots the Chemist Ltd (1996)

More modern roofing materials and installation techniques did not prevent the work being within the covenant to repair.

Creska Ltd v Hammersmith and Fulham London Borough Council (1998)

A more modern design for the underfloor heating system did not prevent the work being within the covenant to repair.

5.8 DEFECT IN DESIGN

As has been noted above, the obligation to keep in repair is not broken unless the subject matter of the covenant is in disrepair. This connotes 'a deterioration from some previous physical condition' or 'a condition worse than it was at some earlier time' (*Post Office v Aquarius Properties Ltd* and *Gibson Investments Ltd v Chesterton plc*). So, a defect in design does not represent disrepair unless there is damage to the subject matter of the covenant.

Quick v Taff-Ely Borough Council (1985)

'When something like this happens, does the landlord or the tenant have a better building? In one sense he does: he gets a building without the design defect which caused the damage; but the repair could only have been done in a sensible way by getting rid of the design defect.'

Is such work reasonably necessary to remedy the damage or the only realistic way of doing so or is it what the sensible man would do? If so, then the work could fall within the covenant to repair.

Gibson Investments Ltd v Chesterton plc (No. 1) (2002)

Where it is contended that the repair work should extend to eradicating the problem, rather than being limited to prophylactic measures, the cases establish, first, that the work will not be repair if it involves giving back to the landlord something wholly different from that which he demised, but, second, there will be circumstances in which such work can be repair even though it involves adding something to the property that was not there originally.

Elmcroft Developments Ltd v Tankersley-Sawyer (1984)

By virtue of the principle highlighted in the two preceding cases, the court in this case concluded that the landlord which had covenanted to keep the main walls of a flat in repair was obliged not only to replace damp plaster but also to insert a damp-proof course to eliminate the cause of the damp.

5.9 COST OF REPAIRS

Also relevant in addition to the nature of the work to be carried out is the potential cost. If it is high when compared with the value of the property and/or the cost of a new building, the chances are that the work will not be within the covenant to repair. Such a result is not inevitable; the cost is merely one of the factors to be taken into account.

Brew Bros Ltd v Snax (Ross) Ltd (1970)

In this case the cost of making safe the flank wall was c. £8,000. The value of the property if in good repair would have been between £7,500 and £9,500. The cost of a new (similar) property on the same plot would have been in the region of £9,000 to £10,000. In the circumstances the court concluded that the work went beyond repair.

Ravenseft Properties Ltd v Davstone (Holdings) Ltd (1979)

The opposite result was reached in this case where the cost of the work (the addition of expansion joints) amounted to c£5,000 and the cost of the work generally was c£55,000. In this case, the work did represent repair.

5.10 WHEN SHOULD A BREACH OF COVENANT BE REMEDIED?

The question then arises: when should the breach of covenant be remedied? The issue was touched on in Chapter 3, *Limitations*.

British Telecommunications plc v Sun Life Assurance Society plc (1996)

A bulge developed in the external walls of the property concerned. These were parts of the property not demised to the tenant. The landlord covenanted to perform the obligations of the tenant in a head lease including an obligation to repair the property. The issue was whether the landlord was in breach of the repairing obligation as soon as the problem arose or only once a reasonable period of time had elapsed after its appearance. The court held that the former was the case. But the position is likely to be different where a landlord's obligation concerns a part of the property that is within the demise to the tenant. The court noted that there is an exception to the general rule identified earlier (there is an immediate duty to put property into repair) where the defect occurs within an area demised. In that case, the landlord only becomes liable under its covenant when it is in possession of knowledge or information about the defect to the extent that a reasonable landlord would consider whether work was required or not but it fails to carry out necessary work with reasonable haste.

As with Chapter 4, one should note that all these matters discussed above should be borne in mind when considering whether or not the covenants as to the form and condition of the property have been satisfied. One will certainly need to have regard to them when carrying out the inevitable inspection of the property.

Again, reference has already been made to the Protocol and the Guidance Note. As explained in the introductory section of this book, it is not within its scope to discuss the practical steps to be taken when considering or responding to dilapidations claims – reference should be made to such publications which contain plenty of practical relevant advice on the subject.

But, obviously, once one has concluded that there has been a breach of the covenants, the fact will generally need to be communicated to the covenantor. That can be done in a number of ways and which is the most appropriate will, as always, depend on the circumstances of the case. It will also depend on the remedy that one considers should be sought.

6
Remedies

Having established the terms of the tenancy, identified the obligations as to the form and condition of the property and that there is a breach of one or more of them, the next step must, obviously, be to consider what action, if any, one should take next. In other words, what you are going to do about it.

Of course, it could be the case that one decides to take no action at all. An obvious example might be where the lease expiry is imminent, the tenant is in breach of covenant but the landlord intends (and there is plenty of evidence of that intention) to demolish the property. In such a case, as the lease expires the landlord's options for enforcement reduce from a range of choices to just one – to make a monetary claim for loss. A claim for damages for disrepair will be subject to section 18(1) of the *Landlord and Tenant Act* 1927 (discussed in detail below) the effect of which would, in this example, be likely to extinguish a claim anyway as a result of the landlord's intention to demolish.

A tenant that is in breach of the lease may choose not to take remedial action for the same reasons, perhaps gambling on the landlord intending to demolish the property.

But, assuming that taking no action is not an option, while a claim should be put together having regard to the objective (in terms of remedy) one wants to achieve, once the 'claim' is initiated, it is usually the case that many dilapidations claims can be resolved by negotiation.

In the next section, the steps preliminary to taking action to enforce the lease are considered. Again, reference has already been made to the Protocol and the Guidance Note. As explained in the introductory section of this book, it is not within the book's scope to discuss the practical steps to be taken when considering or responding to dilapidations claims – reference should be made to such publications which contain plenty of practical relevant advice on the subject. There is practical guidance also in chapter 36 of Dowding and Reynolds and in the *Dilapidations* chapter of RICS Books online service *isurv dispute resolution*. They consider how negotiations might be approached and what practical action a recipient of a claim (mainly the tenant) can take.

As this book is aimed at surveyors, who are not expected to be responsible for the conduct of a dilapidations dispute if it cannot be successfully negotiated, this section will not consider the precise detail of the different dispute resolution processes or the procedures that apply in each of them.

6.1 PRELIMINARY ACTION

6.1.1 Landlord claims

Where there are preliminary steps specific to a particular remedy, they are considered under the relevant section below.

In almost all cases (certainly where a claim is made by the landlord against the tenant) a schedule of dilapidations will have to be prepared.

Even if a schedule of dilapidations is not required for some reason, if there is a prospect that a dispute will become the subject of court proceedings, the guidance given in the *Civil Procedure Rules* 1998 is that steps should be taken to try and resolve the dispute without the need to issue proceedings. Regard must be had, therefore, to the Practice Direction – Protocols set out as part of the *Civil Procedure Rules* 1998. In very brief summary, it encourages the party making the claim to set out a detailed explanation of the claim in a letter supported by any appropriate documents supporting the claim and to invite the recipient to respond in detail, giving the recipient an appropriate period of time to do so.

The schedule of dilapidations can form the basis of a number of types of landlord dilapidations claims, e.g. for damages, for forfeiture, for entry to carry out works, etc. As will be explained below, against each of the items of remedy required, a cost for the work necessary to complete them can be generated, where appropriate. In addition to this, as a separate document, any additional categories of loss can be added to identify the overall claim. The need for and presentation of a claim will be dictated by the remedy being sought. For example, if specific performance is the required remedy, then the development of a claim may not be necessary, as the cost of work should not be an issue. Alternatively, if financial compensation is being sought, then these are important steps, as a loss needs to be proved.

As with the schedule of dilapidations, it is not necessary to follow this slavishly, especially for less complicated claims, but the format adopted must clearly communicate the allegations and the rationale for the losses claimed. The Guidance Note and the Protocol offer guidance as to the format of a schedule of dilapidations. The claim must be laid out so that each element of it, whether construction costs, fees, VAT or other loss, can be seen as a separate item. It is also often useful to include a column for the tenant's response against each item, in a similar manner to the schedule.

The claim may not represent the actual loss to the landlord. The calculation of the loss that the landlord suffers will need to take into account the effect, if any, of the works it actually undertakes on the remedies sought. It will also need to consider, particularly if not all of the works have been completed, whether the effect of the breaches has caused the value of its interest to be reduced, either at all or to the same extent as the claim. This means carrying out a valuation of the diminution of the landlord's interest. While such a valuation may be required if the landlord needs to support an application for permission (under the *Leasehold Property (Repairs) Act 1938*) to seek forfeiture or, during the term of the lease, it is primarily going to be required in a claim for damages at the end of the term. Historically, this was a matter left for the tenant to raise, but with the development of the *Civil Procedure Rules*, this is no longer acceptable. The need for a valuation and the approach to it will be considered in greater depth below under the sections concerning damages claims.

But it is worth noting at this point that the need for a valuation has been emphasised by the Protocol, which came about as a result of the introduction of the *Civil Procedure Rules* 1998 – which themselves had a dramatic effect on the way protagonists behave both before and during proceedings. The effect has been to emphasise the potential need for this additional step in the task of developing the claim; that of determining whether or not the landlord's interest has actually been damaged. To do so, it is first necessary to consider what the landlord is intending to do with the property, and then consider whether this is going to result in the supercession of any items in the claim. With the items that remain, it is then appropriate to consider whether this has caused any diminution in the value of the landlord's interest.

In addition to a schedule of dilapidations, notices may have to be prepared, e.g. to operate the provision of a tenancy to require the tenant to give access to the landlord to inspect the condition of the property and to undertake works that should have been undertaken by the tenant.

6.1.1.1   Service of notices, etc.

Once prepared, the schedule and claim will have to be served. The service of the schedule will be taken as the initiation of the claim. The manner in which the schedule is served will be dictated by the objective the landlord believes it wants to achieve. This involves a consideration of the remedies open to it. These are considered in some depth below, and will therefore only be touched on here, in the context of service. For convenience, service will be considered under each type of remedy, namely:

- damages during the term;
- damages at the end of the term;
- forfeiture;
- the landlord entering and carrying out the works; and
- specific performance.

Wherever a document is to be served, careful consideration should be given to the terms of the tenancy and any express provisions as to service. In some cases, section 196 of the *Law of Property Act* 1925 (which deals with service of notices under that Act, for example, a section 146 notice) is incorporated into or modified by the lease or is simply deemed to apply. Although in some circumstances a notice or document required to be served under the lease can be deemed to have been served even though it will never have reached the intended recipient, one should generally aim to ensure that the document does come to the attention of the intended recipient. Moreover, there are statutory requirements that may have to be satisfied, such as section 18(2) of the *Landlord and Tenant Act 1927*, concerning forfeiture.

Damages during the term

Where a lease was granted for a term of less than seven years or, in the case of a lease granted for more than seven years, there are less than three years of the term remaining, the schedule may simply be served under cover of a suitable letter. The letter and schedule may be accompanied by a summary of the claims made by the landlord. The surveyor should be able to serve these documents.

If the lease was granted for a term of seven years or more and there are more than three years remaining, then the *Leasehold Property (Repairs) Act* 1938 applies and the schedule must be served with a notice given under section 146 of the *Law of Property Act* 1925 containing the form of words required by the 1938 Act. The effect of the 1938 Act is considered separately below. The notice may be served under cover of a suitable letter and the letter and notice may be accompanied by a summary of the claims made by the landlord. Given the technical nature of the documents, they should be served by a solicitor.

Damages at the end of the term

Once the term of the tenancy has expired, there is no other remedy than a claim for damages. Consequently, there is no obligation to serve the schedule other than under cover of a letter, as above. However, care must be taken, because the costs of service may not be recoverable once the term has come to an end, although modern leases usually make it clear that the costs of service are recoverable whether the schedule is served before or after the expiry of the term. The letter and schedule may also be accompanied by a summary of the claims made by the landlord. A surveyor should be able to serve these documents.

Forfeiture

Where a lease was granted for a term of less than seven years or, in the case of a lease granted for more than seven years, there are less than three years of the term remaining, and the landlord intends to threaten to or actually to repossess the building, then the schedule must be served with a notice given under section 146 of the *Law of Property Act* 1925. The notice must be accompanied by a suitable covering letter. Given the technical nature of the documents, they should be served by a solicitor.

If the lease was granted for a term of seven years or more and there are more than three years remaining, then the *Leasehold Property (Repairs) Act* 1938 applies and the schedule must be served with a notice given under section 146 of the *Law of Property Act* 1925, which must contain the form of words required by the 1938 Act. The effect of the 1938 Act is considered separately below. The notice must be accompanied by a suitable covering letter. Again, given the technical nature of the documents, they should be served by a solicitor.

Landlord entering and carrying out works

The landlord's entitlement to enter the building and carry out the work required as a result of the breach of the terms of the tenancy by the tenant and to recover the costs from the tenant depends on the existence of a suitable clause in the lease allowing for this. Such a clause is now commonly known as a *Jervis v Harris* clause (after *Jervis v Harris* – see 2.7). Again, the remedy is further discussed below. However, the main concern of the landlord will be to ensure that the express provisions of the lease concerning service of schedules under the *Jervis v Harris* clause are satisfied. Generally, this will require no more than a suitable letter specifically referring to and complying with any express provisions of the lease. Given the technical nature of the documents required in this instance, they should be served by a solicitor.

Specific performance

Specific performance is a remedy similar to an injunction, i.e. an order requiring the tenant (or the landlord, if it has the maintenance obligations) to carry out the work necessary to comply with the terms as to the condition of the building.

Again, specific performance is considered in greater detail below. There is no need for anything other than a letter notifying the tenant that the works are to be carried out and that specific performance will be sought if they are not. Given the technical nature of the documents required in this instance, they should be served by a solicitor.

However, as specific performance is an entirely discretionary remedy of the court, one should be slow to assume at this stage that it will be ordered. The landlord should consider serving the schedule in a manner that allows it to pursue an alternative course of action.

6.1.2 Tenant claims

Unlike claims by the landlord against the tenant, there are no statutory obligations to be satisfied when initiating a claim against the landlord. There may be contractual obligations to be met and one should always consider the lease to identify whether that is the case and to ensure that they are satisfied.

If the tenant considers that the landlord is at fault in some way, the landlord's covenants should also be scrutinised because it is sometimes the case that the relevant obligation does not take effect unless the landlord has been given appropriate notice. For example, while a covenant to repair causes the covenantor to be in immediate breach (*British Telecommunications plc v Sun Life Assurance Society plc*), if the element of the property in disrepair is within the demise, the landlord should first be given notice (and allowed access) for liability to arise. Without notice in such a case, the landlord will not be at fault.

While there may not be any specific requirements for initiating a claim against the landlord, the points made above concerning general dispute behaviour and the guidance in the *Civil Procedure Rules* 1998 applies equally here.

So, it may be that the tenant should prepare its own form of schedule of the landlord's dilapidations. If the tenant is going to make a claim for damages or for specific performance or carry out the work itself or withhold monies otherwise due to the landlord, it should first give the landlord an appropriate opportunity to remedy its breach. That means setting out the claim and giving the landlord both appropriate time and, if required, access. To do otherwise and then take up one of the options referred to in the preceding sentence could result in the tenant finding itself paying the landlord's costs of any proceedings issued against it and, where the tenant has withheld money, being exposed to a claim, payment of default interest, the levying of distress for non-payment of rent, or forfeiture.

6.2 NEXT STEPS (INCLUDING COURT PROCEEDINGS)

This section will consider the remedies that can be operated where there has been some default by one of the parties to the lease. Primarily they concern those which can be used by the landlord, but they include those available to a tenant (where these are different). It will also consider the restrictions on the remedies. For example, and as mentioned in relation to forfeiture below, the *Insolvency Acts* may prevent action being taken against an individual or company that is insolvent.

The remedies are considered under the following topics:

- forfeiture;
- landlord to enter and carry out works;
- specific performance: landlord's claim against the tenant;
- specific performance: tenant's claim against the landlord;
- damages: landlord's claim against the tenant during the term;
- damages: landlord's claim against the tenant at the end of the term;
- damages: tenant's claim against the landlord;
- tenant to carry out work;
- tenant's set-off (or withholding sums due to the landlord);
- insolvency;
- repudiation and quitting the property; and
- frustration.

6.2.1 Forfeiture

6.2.1.1 General points

Forfeiture is a process by which a landlord can seek to recover possession of a property. In simple terms, it is the result of a breach of the terms of the tenancy, enabling the landlord to assert that it is entitled to regard the tenancy as being at an end (that is, that it is forfeit and no longer exists). Since this is a process by which a tenancy comes to an end, the landlord is entitled to sue on the covenants that come into effect at the end of the term, for example, to yield up the property in good repair.

A tenant faced with forfeiture of a tenancy can generally seek the reinstatement of the lease by a process known as 'relief from forfeiture' (see 6.2.1.6). However, relief (which may be agreed by the landlord or ordered by the court) is usually conditional on the breaches complained of being remedied and the landlord's costs being reimbursed.

Before initiating the forfeiture process, the landlord would be well advised to consider the consequences carefully. By effecting forfeiture, the landlord could find that it achieves possession (which it may not actually want) or that the tenant, to whom a loss of possession might be highly inconvenient, is prompted to carry out the work at its own cost.

If the landlord initiates the forfeiture process and the tenant does not seek relief from forfeiture, or is unsuccessful in its attempt to obtain relief, the landlord cannot undo the process and will find itself with possession of the property. This could prove onerous, with the landlord then becoming liable, for example, for the rates on the property, and also suffering a rental void if the property could not be quickly re-let.

Moreover, during the forfeiture process the landlord may be unable to enforce or operate the covenants in the lease.

6.2.1.2 The forfeiture process

To be able to initiate the forfeiture process, there are certain matters that should be considered:

- Is there a right to forfeit?
- Is there a breach?
- Has the right to forfeit been lost or waived?
- Section 146 notices.

Is there a right to forfeit?

Unless there is a provision allowing the landlord to re-enter the property for breach of covenant, forfeiture cannot be effected. Most leases contain such a right. If the tenancy is not in writing, then apart from considering what the extent of the repairing obligations might be, one will also have to consider whether a right to re-enter was implied into the tenancy. In the case of a yearly tenancy (a tenancy from year to year, often evidenced by the rent being paid yearly), such a provision is implied.

Is there a breach?

This question has been considered above. Unless there is a breach of the covenants concerning the condition of the property, there is no right to forfeit and any attempt to do so will be unlawful and will expose the landlord to a claim by the tenant for damages for any disturbance or losses suffered.

Has the right to forfeit been lost or waived?

Where a landlord has the right to forfeit a lease, it must decide whether or not to do so. If it chooses not to forfeit, then the lease will continue, although the landlord may be able to seek some other remedy.

As forfeiture operates to bring the tenancy to an end, the landlord and tenant relationship will also be at an end if forfeiture is effected. Therefore, if the landlord carries on in a manner that can only be consistent with the continued existence of that relationship, it follows that the tenancy cannot be at an end. If there was a right to forfeit, the landlord will be deemed to have lost or waived that right. A typical example of how the right might be lost is by the demand or acceptance of rent due on a date after the landlord had knowledge of the breach giving rise to the entitlement to forfeit.

The law has also modified the concept of waiver and has developed the concept of what are known as one-off and continuing breaches. Where there is a one-off breach, then the right to forfeit as a result of it can be readily lost by, say, the demand or acceptance of rent due on a date after the landlord had knowledge of the breach and was aware that it gave rise to a right to forfeit. An example of a one-off breach might be the carrying-out of alterations contrary to the terms of the lease.

Where there is a continuing breach, then a new breach is deemed to occur every day. Thus, the demand or acceptance of rent due on a date after the landlord had knowledge of the breach giving rise to a right to forfeit will not waive the right to forfeit provided that the breach remains in existence or becomes worse. An example of a continuing breach would be a breach of the covenant to repair.

While it is commonly thought that in dilapidations cases waiver of the right to forfeit is of limited relevance, care must still be taken, as some of the covenants broken might give rise to a one-off breach, for example, a covenant to decorate by a certain date. Consequently, the cautious landlord will immediately stop demanding and collecting rent or otherwise dealing with the tenant under the lease until it has consulted its lawyers and carefully considered its position and the action it might take.

If, as a result of the forfeiture and a delay in the grant of relief from forfeiture, the landlord cannot operate some provision of the lease without risking waiving the right to forfeit, the court will generally take the view that the landlord should not suffer as a result of the default of the tenant and will allow the provision to be operated late or retrospectively.

Section 146 notices

For forfeiture to occur, a notice under section 146 of the *Law of Property Act* 1925 must be served. A landlord is not entitled to forfeit a tenancy (other than for non-payment of rent) unless it has first served a notice under that section. A section 146 notice is a technical document and should be drafted and served by the landlord's lawyer.

In simple terms, the section 146 notice should:

- particularise the parties to the lease;
- identify the current landlord and tenant;
- set out or summarise the relevant terms of the lease;

- explain the breach complained of;
- if the breach is capable of remedy, invite the tenant to remedy the breach within a reasonable time; and
- require the tenant to pay compensation to the landlord.

As noted, the notice should require the tenant to remedy the breach. One would include such provision even if the breach is incapable of remedy. A classic example of such a breach of covenant is when a tenant sublets without having obtained the prior consent of the landlord (assuming that it was required by the lease). What is the position in the context of dilapidations? An obvious relevant and similar covenant is that prohibiting alterations without first having obtained the landlord's consent.

Savva and another v Houssein (1996)

This case concerned a claim for forfeiture where it was alleged that unlawful alterations had been carried out. It was also contended, on behalf of the tenant, that the section 146 notice was defective because, if the breaches complained of were capable of remedy, the notice should have required remedy (which it did not).

> 'When something has been done without consent, it is not possible to restore the matter wholly to the situation which it was in before the breach ... it is a remedy if the mischief caused by the breach can be removed. In the case of a covenant not to make alterations without consent or not to display signs without consent, if there is a breach of that, the mischief can be removed by removing the signs or restoring the property to the state it was in before the alterations ... all the breaches complained of in this case were capable of remedy. It follows that the notice under section 146 should have required them to be remedied.'

Where the *Leasehold Property (Repairs) Act* 1938 applies, the section 146 notice must also contain a statement in characters no less conspicuous than those used in any other part of the notice specifying that the Act applies; noting that the tenant is entitled to serve a counter-notice under the Act; noting the manner in which and the date by which that counter-notice must be served; and giving the name and address of the landlord. (The Act is considered briefly in 6.2.1.3 below.)

Again, as such a notice is a technical document, it should be drafted and served by the landlord's lawyer. If forfeiture is contemplated, the section 146 notice must be served in compliance with section 18(2) of the *Landlord and Tenant Act* 1927.

6.2.1.3 The Leasehold Property (Repairs) Act 1938

The 1938 Act applies to leases granted for a term of seven years or more and in respect of which there are three years or more left unexpired at the point at which the notice is served. It applies to breaches of the repairing covenant (properly so called). It does not apply to breaches of similar covenants, for example, to decorate, but one may have to decorate as part of the covenant to repair. It applies where a landlord is proposing to forfeit the lease or to seek damages during the term of the lease.

With regard to forfeiture, where the 1938 Act applies, and the tenant (which does not include a mortgagee in possession – as in *Smith v Spaul* (2003)), within 28 days of service of the section 146 notice, serves a counter-notice taking the benefit of the Act, the landlord may not proceed with forfeiture (or a damages claim) without first obtaining the permission of the court.

There are five grounds under the 1938 Act on which the court can give permission:

1   when the immediate remedying of the breach in question is requisite for preventing substantial diminution in the value of the landlord's reversion, or that the value thereof has been substantially diminished by the breach;

2   when the immediate remedying of the breach is required for giving effect in relation to the property to the purposes of any enactment, or of any by-law or other provision having effect under an enactment, or for giving effect to any order of a court or requirement of any authority under any enactment or any such by-law or other provision as aforesaid;

3   in a case in which the tenant is not in occupation of the whole of the property with regard to which the covenant or agreement is proposed to be enforced, and where the

immediate remedying of the breach is required in the interests of the occupier of the property or of part thereof;

4   when the breach can be immediately remedied at an expense that is relatively small in comparison with the much greater expense that would probably be occasioned by postponement of the necessary work; or

5   in special circumstances which, in the opinion of the court, render it just and equitable that permission should be given.

Landmaster Properties Ltd v Thackeray Property Service Ltd (2003)

Generally, the time at which the landlord will have to prove the ground(s) upon which it relies will be the date of the hearing of the application for permission.

Clearly, careful consideration must be given to each of the grounds. Only one needs to be satisfied for the court to be able to exercise its discretion to give permission to proceed. If the 1938 Act applies and permission is to be sought, the proceedings seeking permission will have to be accompanied by appropriate evidence supporting the ground to be relied upon.

6.2.1.4   Other restrictions on forfeiture

Under various statutes, there are restrictions on forfeiture (or other enforcement action). The most notable in the context of dilapidations with regard to commercial property are contained in the *Insolvency Acts* and related Acts. If the tenant is insolvent and has become bankrupt, or has gone into liquidation, or has entered into an individual or company voluntary arrangement, or has gone into administration under an Administration Order, then care should be taken before proceeding with any enforcement action and specialist advice should be sought.

6.2.1.5   Effecting forfeiture

Assuming that the restrictions on forfeiture have been satisfied, or do not apply, and that a reasonable time has elapsed since the service of the section 146 notice, then the landlord may proceed to forfeit the lease. This may be effected by one of two methods: peaceable re-entry or court proceedings.

Peaceable re-entry

Often evidenced by changing the locks to the property, forfeiture by peaceable re-entry requires an unequivocal act by the landlord demonstrating that it has exercised its right to forfeit the lease. It can also sometimes be achieved by re-letting the property.

In practice, peaceable re-entry is often effected by the instruction of certificated bailiffs, who attend the property in the early hours of the morning before the tenant or the occupiers of the property have arrived for work. In this way, the landlord is more likely to avoid the difficulties of encountering someone at the property who is opposed to the re-entry. To use or threaten violence against someone in those circumstances is a criminal offence under the *Criminal Law Act* 1977.

The main advantage of forfeiting by peaceable re-entry is that the forfeiture is immediate and the costs of court proceedings are potentially avoided. However, if the tenant is generally in occupation, the landlord can run the risk of a substantial claim for damages if the tenant is deemed to have been put out of occupation unlawfully (there might be a large amount of business lost, or damage to the tenant's goodwill). In those circumstances, although it is not uncommon for surveyors to instruct certificated bailiffs to forfeit a lease, the landlord should be encouraged to consult its lawyers first.

It is unlawful to forfeit otherwise than by proceedings if the property is let as a dwelling and someone is lawfully residing in it (section 2 of the *Protection from Eviction Act* 1977). To effect peaceable re-entry, it is therefore necessary to consider what the primary purpose of the letting was.

Court proceedings

If there is any doubt about the primary purpose of the letting, or if someone is in residential occupation or is in occupation resisting the recovery of possession, making it difficult or unlawful to re-enter, then court proceedings will be the better or only method of forfeiting the lease.

Ivory Gate Ltd v Spetale (1998)

The issue and service of forfeiture proceedings does not represent the forfeiture, but once served, they do operate as evidence of the landlord's unequivocal election to forfeit the tenancy.

As a result of the possibility of relief from forfeiture being available, the *Civil Procedure Rules* require copies of the proceedings (in the case of residential property) to be served on those who may be entitled to seek that relief, such as mortgagees or subtenants. The relevant *Civil Procedure Rules* provision does not seem to apply to commercial property, but as a landlord will want to ensure that any forfeiture order is not unravelled by the later involvement of a subtenant or mortgagee, it is good practice to serve copies of the proceedings on them. Although there is no procedural requirement to that effect, there may be an express term of the tenancy to do so.

As a surveyor will not be issuing or conducting such proceedings, they will not be considered further in this book.

Once forfeiture has been effected and the landlord has gained possession of the property, it is free to deal with the property as it sees fit. However, there may be other persons or organisations with an interest in it, who might be able to seek relief from forfeiture.

If the lease that has been forfeit was granted before 13 October 2003 and was for a term of more than 21 years, it will have been (or ought to have been) registered at the Land Registry, with a leasehold title. If this is the case, then before a new lease can be granted (particularly if it is also to be of a registerable term), the leasehold title must be closed. This requires an application to the Land Registry, supported by evidence that the lease has been forfeited.

Since 13 October 2003, the position has altered slightly, as a result of the implementation of the *Land Registration Act* 2002. New leases granted for a term of more than seven years must be registered and, where an old lease having more than seven years remaining on the term is assigned, the lease must now be registered on the assignment, even though it was originally granted before 13 October 2003 and was for a term of 21 years or less.

6.2.1.6 Relief from forfeiture

Where a landlord has forfeited or is seeking to forfeit a lease, the tenant may be entitled to seek relief from forfeiture. Moreover, any subtenant or mortgagee of the tenant may be entitled to seek such relief.

Although there are various provisions concerning relief from forfeiture, where the breach is of the terms as to the condition of the property, the tenant, subtenant or mortgagee may only seek relief from forfeiture under section 146 of the *Law of Property Act* 1925 (the position is different in relation to non-payment of rent).

An application may be made as soon as the section 146 notice has been served and may be made even though the landlord has forfeited by peaceable re-entry. If forfeiture is effected by court proceedings, then an application must be made before the landlord executes any order for possession. If the order has been executed and the landlord has actually recovered possession, then the right to relief from forfeiture in these circumstances is lost. Moreover, the court has discretion as to whether and how it grants relief from forfeiture such that any application should be made swiftly.

The court also has discretion as to the terms of relief from forfeiture. More often than not, it will make relief conditional upon the tenant or other applicant carrying out the work necessary to remedy the breaches for which forfeiture has been effected. This is not always the case, however, and there will be (perhaps limited) circumstances where relief is given without that condition. If new breaches have occurred since the forfeiture was effected, then the court might also require those to be remedied. The court will also generally require the tenant to reimburse the landlord for the costs that it has incurred as a result of the breaches and to provide any compensation for losses that would not be resolved by the tenant doing the works.

There is a great deal of complexity surrounding the status of the tenancy in the period between the commencement and service of forfeiture proceedings and the hearing of the tenant's application for relief from forfeiture. Although the forfeiture is not confirmed until the eventual court order, it becomes effective as at the date of service of the proceedings. If the tenant's application for relief is successful, then in most circumstances relief is effective as at the service of proceedings. In the interim period, however, it would seem that the landlord may have difficulty enforcing some or all of the terms of the tenancy. However, if there are breaches of the terms of the tenancy during that period, then once relief is achieved, those breaches may be retrospectively enforced.

Given all these issues and complexities, a surveyor acting for a tenant, subtenant or mortgagee should encourage the client to seek legal advice as soon as possible after a section 146 notice has been served.

6.2.2 Landlord to enter and carry out works

This remedy flows from an entitlement under the lease in favour of the landlord to enter the property demised to the tenant to carry out works that it should have undertaken but has failed to do. There is a detailed discussion of such obligations in Chapter 2, *Frequently encountered covenants and lease provisions*.

In this chapter, the subject is discussed below under the following topics:

- general points (including discussion of *Jervis v Harris* clauses);
- the notice;
- the entry and works;
- access refused;
- demand and enforcement.

6.2.2.1 General points

As discussed earlier in this book, most modern leases contain a clause enabling a landlord to enter the property, inspect it for compliance by the tenant with the terms of the tenancy concerning the condition of the property, give a notice to the tenant requiring it to carry out the work required within a specified period of time, and indicating that, in default, the landlord will enter the property, carry out the work and seek to recover the cost of doing so from the tenant. As mentioned above, such clauses have become known as *Jervis v Harris* clauses.

As most leases contain such a clause, this section will only consider these. However, it should be remembered that there may be instances where there is no such clause. Theoretically, the landlord will not be able to enter in the manner described above; however, legal advice should be sought because, in practice, there may be lawful means of achieving a similar, but not as complete, result.

Where there is an appropriate clause allowing the landlord to enter to carry out the work necessitated by the tenant's breach of the terms of the tenancy, then there are usually conditions that must be satisfied first. The terms of the tenancy must be carefully considered to ensure that such conditions are met.

6.2.2.2 The notice

When the necessary notice is served, it must satisfy any express terms of the tenancy. In addition, it should avoid specifying the remedial work to be carried out. There are often a number of ways of remedying a breach, and the landlord could find that it has specified an inappropriate method or that the tenant carries out the work in a different manner, leaving the way open for a dispute about whether or not it has complied with the notice.

6.2.2.3 The entry and works

If a proper notice has been given and the tenant has failed to comply with it, the landlord may then enter the property, but only to carry out the works specified in the notice and in accordance with the tenant's covenants concerning the condition of the property. Therefore, although it is not impossible that additional work may be carried out, such a situation will be rare. Consequently, the landlord's original inspection should be as complete as possible and the notice should be as full as possible as to the defects complained of.

Bearing in mind that there may be more than one way of remedying a breach, and although the failure by the tenant to comply with the notice results in it losing its ability to choose the appropriate method, the landlord should be careful to limit its choice of method to one that is reasonable and preferably to one that is most favourable to the tenant. The landlord would also be well advised to ensure that it does not stay at the property for an unreasonable period of time, that the cost of the work is reasonable and that it is carried out to a reasonable standard. It should also ensure that no damage is caused to the tenant by the carrying out of the works (beyond, one would suggest, the damage that the tenant would have itself endured had it done the requisite work itself). Otherwise, there may be a later dispute when the landlord seeks to recover the cost of carrying out the work from the tenant.

In addition, the landlord will need to be careful not to break the 'quiet enjoyment' covenant that it will have either expressly or by implication given to the tenant. It is extremely easy for the landlord to overstep the mark, either by carrying out work that is not part of the tenant's obligations, carrying out work which has not been originally specified, or allowing its contractor, possibly involuntarily, to breach the landlord's covenant for quiet enjoyment. This is particularly tricky in the case of services required by the contractors and which the tenant may not be obligated to provide.

Goldmile Properties Ltd v Lechouritis (2003)

As this case illustrates, notwithstanding that the landlord may be entitled to enter the property and carry out the work, it must take all reasonable steps not to unduly interfere with the tenant's enjoyment of the property.

6.2.2.4 Access refused

If the tenant declines to give access, then the only options for the landlord are to seek an injunction from the court by which the court will order the tenant to give access, or to take forfeiture action (if this is possible), having first served a section 146 notice.

Hammersmith & Fulham London Borough Council v Creska (No. 2) (2000)

An injunction is a discretionary remedy and will not always be granted. In some circumstances, the court might consider the landlord's right to be oppressive, as in this case, especially when considering the nature and extent of the tenant's breach complained of. It might consider that the landlord can be adequately compensated in damages (i.e. by the payment of a sum of money).

6.2.2.5 Demand and enforcement

Once the landlord has gained access and has carried out the work, it can make a demand of the tenant for reimbursement of the costs incurred.

The advantage of this for the landlord is that it avoids the effect of the *Leasehold Property (Repairs) Act* 1938 and section 18(1) of the *Landlord and Tenant Act* 1927 (see 6.2.6, 'Damages: landlord's claim against the tenant at the end of the term'). Moreover, in practice the threat of this often results in the tenant carrying out the work without the landlord having to do so itself. The motivation for the tenant is that it retains control of the manner in which the work is carried out and its cost.

The disadvantage is that if the landlord actually carries out the work, it has to 'forward fund' the work, and may not be able to recover the cost from an impecunious tenant.

Although the landlord may be able to forfeit the tenancy as a consequence, that may not be a desirable result. If the cost of the work is recoverable as a debt, an alternative remedy might be to bankrupt or wind up the tenant under the *Insolvency Acts*, but that might lead to the recovery of possession which is not always what the landlord wishes to achieve.

The 1938 Act is considered in section 6.2.1.3, on forfeiture. Until 1996 there was debate about whether the Act applied to any claim for forfeiture or money that the landlord might make having exercised the *Jervis v Harris* clause. However, in *Jervis v Harris*, it was held that the landlord's claim was not a claim for damages, but for a debt. As a consequence, the 1938 Act was held not to apply. If the clause refers to the tenant paying 'damages', then the 1938 Act might apply. Most modern leases do not describe the landlord's costs in that way, however, but as payable on demand (i.e. as a debt).

Section 18(1) of the 1927 Act has also been mentioned briefly above, and will be considered in greater depth in 6.2.6.2. As noted above, the effect of the section is to place a cap on the level of damages a landlord can seek to recover from a tenant in default of the repairing terms of the tenancy.

Although *Jervis v Harris* was concerned with the 1938 Act, it is difficult to see any reason why the principle should not equally apply to section 18(1) of the 1927 Act, such that it will not operate to limit the landlord's claim made under the *Jervis v Harris* clause. As a consequence, subject to the landlord being willing to forward fund the work, the landlord could have the work carried out late on in the term of the tenancy, effectively at the tenant's expense, without having to deal with section 18(1).

6.2.3 Specific performance: landlord's claim against the tenant

Specific performance as a remedy available to a landlord was mentioned when the service of the schedule of dilapidations was considered in 6.1, 'Preliminary action'. It is a remedy similar to an injunction, i.e. an order requiring the tenant (or landlord, if it has the maintenance obligations) to carry out the work necessary to comply with the terms as to the condition of the property. In other words, it is an order requiring someone to do what was promised.

Rainbow Estates Ltd v Tokenhold Ltd (1999)

While there had been some doubt about the availability of the remedy to a landlord, a claim by a landlord for specific performance of the repairing covenants by a tenant was permitted. Although this was a first instance decision, to date there has been no contrary case.

Specific performance is a discretionary remedy (like an injunction) and will generally only be ordered if it is just and equitable to do so. It is less likely to be ordered, therefore, if the landlord can be adequately compensated by the payment of damages or if there are other suitable remedies available to the landlord, such as forfeiture. If the lease does not contain a *Jervis v Harris* clause, however, then specific performance may be ordered.

As a general rule, the court will veer against making an order that cannot be specific as to what can be done or that will require it, effectively, to supervise the action required to be carried out. Therefore, the work to be done must be the subject of a clear schedule. The court will also take care to ensure that specific performance is not being used to avoid some other restriction on the landlord to enforce the terms of the tenancy, such as the obligations of the *Leasehold Property (Repairs) Act* 1938. Therefore, and as mentioned in the *Rainbow Estates* case, one can expect the court to have regard to the 1938 Act when considering whether or not to order specific performance and when seeking to satisfy itself that the landlord has legitimate reasons for requiring the tenant to carry out the works.

If the landlord delays in seeking specific performance, then the court will take that into consideration when deciding whether or not to make the order. The longer and the more inexcusable the delay, the less likely it is that an order will be made. The possibility of the tenant being caused hardship is another factor. Where the lease does not have long to run, the court will be slow to order specific performance, particularly if the work cannot be carried out before the end of the term.

If the court does order the tenant to carry out the work by way of specific performance, then as with the breach of an injunction, the failure to do so will constitute contempt of court and the court may order that the tenant (or a director of the tenant where it is a company) be imprisoned. The court may also order the landlord to carry out the work and recover the cost from the tenant.

6.2.4 Specific performance: tenant's claim against the landlord

The principles of specific performance by a landlord of its obligations with regard to the condition of the property are more or less the same as those described above in the context of a claim by a landlord against a tenant.

The most likely difficulty for a tenant arises where the tenant does not have full access to the area of the property in respect of which it says that the landlord has failed to meet its obligations. Consequently, while the tenant will need to provide a schedule of the work the landlord should carry out, it may be that the schedule will be less detailed than an equivalent schedule where a landlord is seeking to enforce a tenant's obligations. However, it may be the case that the landlord can be assumed to be aware of what is required of it.

Obviously, the restrictions under, say, the *Leasehold Property (Repairs) Act* 1938 have no application in a claim by a tenant against a landlord. Nonetheless, the remedy of specific performance remains discretionary and will only be exercised by the court if it is just and equitable in all the circumstances. Alternatively, the court may simply order the landlord to pay damages.

6.2.5 Damages: landlord's claim against the tenant during the term

As mentioned above, the *Leasehold Property (Repairs) Act* 1938 can apply to a landlord's claim for damages during the term of the tenancy. However, even if the tenancy was granted for a term of seven years or more, the 1938 Act will not apply if there are less than three years of the term remaining.

If the 1938 Act applies, then the question of forfeiture may be relevant. See 6.2.1 concerning forfeiture for a summary of how this affects a claim and the steps that must be taken to comply with it.

Whether the 1938 Act applies or not, the approach to the quantification of damages that a landlord might claim of a tenant who has broken the terms of a tenancy concerning the condition of the property will be the same.

The measure of damages that a landlord can claim against a tenant during the term of the tenancy is effectively the same whether under case law or statute: namely, the amount by which the landlord's reversion has been diminished by the breaches. Although the cost of the works necessary to remedy the breaches may be an indicator of the diminution in value of the landlord's reversion, it is nothing more than that.

The statutory provision that limits a claim for damages made both during and after the term is section 18(1) of the *Landlord and Tenant Act* 1927. As that section only confirms the position arrived at by case law, and as it has a greater effect on claims for damages made at or after the end of the tenancy, it will be considered in greater depth in the next section – 6.2.6, 'Damages: landlord's claim against the tenant at the end of the term'.

The factors to be considered when trying to assess the damages suffered by a landlord for a breach by the tenant during the term are, among other things, as follows:

(i)   The amount of the term remaining. If the tenancy has a very long time to run, the damage to the reversion is likely to be minimal, particularly as any hypothetical purchaser would be able to enforce the terms of the tenancy. However, if the term has almost run out, there may be little difference between the amount of damages that might be sought during the term and those sought at the end of the term.

(ii) Is the landlord liable to third parties? If so, there may be substantial diminution to the reversion.

(iii) Does the tenant have security of tenure under, for example, Part II of the *Landlord and Tenant Act* 1954 (which gives protection to business tenants)? If so, and as the new business tenancy can be expected to contain similar obligations concerning the condition of the property to those in the existing lease, there may be limited damage to the reversion.

(iv) Is the landlord going to, or can it, carry out the work? If not, then that might suppress its claim.

(v)   Is the landlord itself a tenant? If so, that may have an impact on the claim.

The date at which the claim is valued depends on the circumstances. The general rule is that damages are assessed as at the date of the breach; however, in dilapidations cases, the damages are more likely to be assessed at the date of the hearing. If the term of the tenancy expires before the hearing, then it is more likely than not that damages will be assessed as at the expiry of the tenancy.

An obvious disadvantage of a damages claim during the term is that it will not necessarily result in the works being carried out, and the need to comply with the 1938 Act may complicate matters. As a result, stand-alone claims for damages during the term are uncommon. It is more likely that a claim for damages will be added to a claim for forfeiture or for specific performance.

6.2.6 Damages: landlord's claim against the tenant at the end of the term

In practice, the majority of dilapidations claims relate to the landlord's claim against the tenant at the end of the term. Since the tenant no longer has a right to occupy the property and therefore perform the covenants (nor can the landlord operate remedies such as the right to enter), such claims can only be for damages and one is required to consider the appropriate manner of assessing the landlord's loss, i.e. whether the damages should be the actual cost of repairs or whether the claim is capped by the amount by which the landlord's interest has diminished in value.

This assessment is a fundamental part of a damages claim for dilapidations at the end of the term of the tenancy; there are a considerable number of issues to be taken into account and a number of approaches available. These are therefore reviewed in a separate subsection, the valuation of damages.

Particularly relevant in a claim for damages at the end of the term is the condition of the property at that point. The prudent landlord and tenant should have a record of condition made as the lease expires in the hope that, should there be a dispute about the matter at some later point, there is some evidence available.

6.2.6.1 The valuation of damages

As mentioned in section 6.2.5, concerning a landlord's claim for damages during the term, the approach to the quantification of damages is greatly affected by section 18(1) of the 1927 Act.

6.2.6.2 General points

For further guidance as to how to approach a landlord's claim for damages for dilapidations at the end of the term, see the Protocol and the Guidance Note.

There are no procedural restrictions on making a claim for damages at the end of the term. Thus, for example, there is no need for a section 146 notice (see 6.2.1, 'Forfeiture') and there is no need to seek the court's permission to make a claim under the *Leasehold Property (Repairs) Act* 1938.

The measure of damages under case law (known as common law damages) is the proper cost of works plus associated losses (for example, the loss of rent while the work is carried out). This is commented on in more detail in 6.2.6.5. It is worth noting, however, that there will be circumstances where the reasonable approach to the assessment of common law loss is on the difference in value of the property (or a specific item concerned) in repair and out of repair. In other words, a common law claim could be the damage to the reversion (see 6.2.6.11, 'Non-section 18(1) losses').

Of greater significance to a claim for damages at the end of the term is section 18(1) of the 1927 Act, which has been mentioned above briefly on a number of occasions. Given its significance, it is set out in full:

Crown copyright material is reproduced with the permission of the Controller of HMSO and the Queen's Printer for Scotland.

'Damages for a breach of a covenant or agreement to keep or put premises in repair during the currency of a lease, or to leave or put premises in repair at the termination of a lease, whether such covenant or agreement is expressed or implied, and whether general or specific, shall in no case exceed the amount (if any) by which the value of the reversion (whether immediate or not) in the premises is diminished owing to the breach of such covenant or agreement as aforesaid; and in particular no damage shall be recovered for a breach of any such covenant or agreement to leave or put premises in repair at the termination of a lease, if it is shown that the premises, in whatever state of repair they might be, would at or shortly after the termination of the tenancy have been or be pulled down, or such structural alterations made therein as would render valueless the repairs covered by the covenant or agreement.'

Section 18(1) can be divided into two parts, known as 'limbs'. The first limb imposes a statutory 'ceiling' on the damages payable, being the lesser of the cost of works (common law damages) and the diminution in the value of the landlord's reversion at the valuation date (statutory damages – a discussion of the assessment of statutory damages can be found at 6.2.6.8–6.2.6.10). The second limb extinguishes entirely the landlord's right to claim damages for breach of the repairing covenant at the expiry of the term if it intends to demolish or substantially alter the property.

Section 18(1) only applies to covenants to repair, properly so called. There could be some claims that might be made under other covenants (such as the covenant to decorate), which are not covered by section 18(1).

It is accepted that where it is clear that the section 18(1) limit will operate, in practice one might not seek to quantify the damages (i.e. costing the works of repair) other than to assess the damage to the reversion. However, usually it will be necessary to proceed down both routes in order to ascertain which will provide the lower level of damages.

Section 18(1): the first limb

As mentioned above, section 18(1) only applies to covenants to repair; it does not apply to other covenants (such as covenants to decorate), even if they are contained in the repairing covenant. In simple terms, this means that a surveyor advising a landlord will have to analyse the works and split them into two categories: those to which section 18(1) applies and those to which it does not. Then, in relation to those to which it does apply, the surveyor must compare them with the damage to the value of the reversion resulting from the breach by the tenant. If the damage to the reversion is less than the cost of works to remedy the breaches of the true repairing covenants, that is the limit on that part of the landlord's claim. This was aptly illustrated in the conclusion of the judgment in *Mason v Totalfinaelf UK Ltd*.

Mason v Totalfinaelf UK Ltd (2003)

'I accept that if, and to the extent that, he is put in funds, Mr Mason intends to carry out the various items of repair that have been the subject of agreement between the parties or that I have found to be breaches of Total's repairing obligations. I find that, inclusive of the agreed items, the overall cost of the works needed to make good the breaches amounts to £120,302, to which, as was common ground, a further 12% falls to be added for surveyors' supervising fees. This produces an overall figure of £134,738. Since, however, the diminution in value of the freehold (Mr Mason's reversionary interest) was £73,500, it follows that his claim for damages succeeds but is capped at that figure.'

Simmons v Dresden (2004)

This case highlighted a number of important points concerning dilapidations claims:

- that even though the landlord may have excellent professional advice from expert building and valuation surveyors, the court can still decide against it, reducing the claim significantly (in this case, effectively to nil);

- that the court can choose to disregard expert valuation evidence if it finds it not to be of assistance to it;

- that the parties will need to take care to adduce evidence to support their assertions, otherwise the court could disallow such claims;

- that it is for the landlord to prove that the value of its reversion had been diminished by the disrepair; and

- given the number of individual items frequently in dispute in addition to more substantial issues, dilapidations claims are very expensive to pursue.

However, if in practice the landlord does not carry out or intend to carry out the repairs, reinstatement or decorations to the property, then whether one is considering statutory damages under section 18, or common law damages, it is possible that these will amount to the same thing. This is because the cost of works (common law damages) will only be appropriate, at the end of the term, if the landlord has carried out or there is a likelihood that it will carry out the works. Pragmatically therefore, one could carry out a valuation for diminution in value to cover all of the breaches.

Section 18(1): the second limb

The second limb of section 18(1) states that no claim will succeed if it can be shown that shortly after the termination of the lease, whatever the state of repair, the property is to be pulled down or so significantly structurally altered that it will render the repairs valueless. It is important to look at the position from the viewpoint of the landlord's intentions at or around the end of the lease. It is possible for the landlord to decide to carry out the dilapidation remedial works, but subsequently to change its mind and undertake substantial works, and not fall foul of the second limb of section 18(1). However, if, for example, there was a valid planning permission in place or returned tenders at the termination of the lease, it will be difficult for the landlord to prove that it was not its intention to carry out the substantial scheme, irrespective of the applicable dates.

6.2.6.3 Landlord's intentions

The loss to the landlord caused by the tenant's non-compliance with the provisions of the lease will be affected and, in some cases, defined, by the landlord's intention at and immediately after the end of the lease, and by its subsequent actions (as in *Salisbury (Marquess) v Gilmore* (1942)).

In some instances, a landlord may be undecided as to its intentions, but this does not preclude the obligation on the tenant to settle its liabilities.

Cunliffe v Goodman (1950)

The period during which the landlord was considering what it would do with the building was described as the 'zone of contemplation'.

Once the landlord has settled upon a course of action, the plans under consideration move out of the zone of contemplation and into the 'valley of decision'. How long that period (i.e. between the commencement of the consideration of a plan of action and settling on it) might last is a matter of fact and degree, but it will not go on indefinitely. After that period, if the landlord has not made up its mind and fixed its intention, the court will infer that its intention at or immediately after the end of the lease was to do nothing, and any actions after that point in time will be deemed subsequent changes of intention. If, however, within a relatively short time after the end of the lease, the landlord decides to carry out the works, this will probably still be the correct measure of its loss.

Where a landlord is seeking damages for the breaches, it ought to state what its intentions are as part of its claim, so that the tenant has the opportunity to consider the effect of them on the claim. In situations where the need for a diminution valuation is deferred, it is probably legitimate for the tenant to defer the analysis of the claim against it, as the landlord's losses will not be capable of proof. Where a landlord has made a clear decision contemporary with the end of the lease to take a particular course of action, but then has a change of heart, it is likely to be bound by the first decision (as in *Salisbury (Marquess) v Gilmore* (1942)). It is particularly important, therefore, for the landlord to be clear and truthful about its intentions.

However, if the landlord is unable to decide for more than a few months, or fails to start the works for a similar time, it is likely that its claim for the consequential losses (see 6.2.6.6) will fail. This is because any loss of rent, or other similar matters, will become insignificant when compared with the losses flowing from its own indecision.

Supercession

A similar approach can be applied to individual items of claim if the landlord's intentions would negate or supersede the work said to be necessary to remedy the breach of the lease complained of. For example, where there is disrepair to a heating system, but the landlord decides to renew, rather than repair, the boilers, so that it can provide a system with a reasonable life expectancy for re-letting, then while the repair to the radiators and pipework would be valid, the cost of the new boilers could not be claimed. This principle is called 'supercession' and it is for this reason that the tenant should ask what the landlord's intentions for the property are.

Therefore, once the landlord's intentions have been determined, it is necessary to consider what items of work, that the landlord contends should have been carried out by the tenant, if any, are superseded as a result. If there are substantial differences between the works to be undertaken by the landlord and those included in the dilapidations claim, then it is likely that the effect of supercession will be substantial. To make the assessment, the implications of the landlord's intentions need to be compared with each item of the schedule. Where an item is negated or modified by the work to be carried out by the landlord, this should be stated. Where this analysis is more complicated, it may be appropriate to include an additional column in the schedule of dilapidations, so that this step can be seen separately.

6.2.6.4 The Protocol

Owing to the dual approach to the assessment of damages, the Protocol states that where a landlord does not intend to undertake the works, at an appropriate time it ought to provide a diminution in value calculation in the initial claim for dilapidations. Similarly, if the landlord intends to undertake the work, but has not yet done so, it ought to state what steps have been taken towards completing the work (such as preparing specifications or obtaining tenders).

However, as only the landlord knows what it intends to do with a property at the expiry of a lease, it is only right that the landlord 'lays all his cards on the table' if it does not propose to do the works. If the landlord is encouraged to provide a diminution in value calculation (which until recently has been considered a tenant's defence), it may also encourage the landlord to be more open in its discussions with the tenant concerning the future of the property. It is often the case that a property is ripe for development and that such development would nullify any claim by the landlord for dilapidations, but because of the landlord's reluctance to indicate its intentions, a lengthy and possibly unnecessary negotiation and litigation process has ensued.

6.2.6.5 Assessing loss at common law

The amount of damages recoverable at common law for breach of the repairing covenant is frequently the amount properly payable to return the property to the condition in which it would have been if the tenant had complied with its covenants to repair, in addition to other allowable items. One must not forget that on occasion the correct approach will be to assess the diminution in value (see *Ruxley Electronics & Construction Ltd v Forsyth* discussed in section 6.2.6.11).

This measure of damages was laid down in the case of *Joyner v Weeks*.

Joyner v Weeks (1891)

Although the court concluded that the cost of works was the proper measure of damages, it is interesting to note that the lower court (which was overruled on the point) had decided that the measure should be diminution in the value of the reversion not exceeded by the cost of works – a position that anticipated and led to the implementation of section 18(1).

6.2.6.6 Heads of loss

The heads of loss that are often encountered in a claim for common law damages can be summarised as follows:

- cost of works;
- consequential losses, such as loss of rent;
- fees;
- interest on finance;
- other occupational costs; and
- VAT.

General points

Many dilapidations claims are based on losses that the landlords have actually incurred; that is, they have done the work, paid their contractors and incurred the time that this took.

Joyner v Weeks (1891)

On the face of it, as explained above, the evidence as to the landlord's loss will be the costs that it has actually incurred in carrying out work that was the responsibility of the tenant.

Cost of works

Although the costs of works is the primary evidence in a claim, it is not always a fair indication of a loss. For example, the costs may have been incurred at non-market rates or based on inappropriate methods of execution of work. However, if the cost has been reasonably incurred, it is difficult to argue that it is not the appropriate measure of loss. As the landlord will have assumed the risk of completing the works, it is likely that the court will consider that the cost of the works is the measure of the loss, and the 'diminution in value' defences will fail. In situations where the work has not been executed, it is necessary to project what the costs might be. If quotations for the works have been obtained, then these will typically be the best measure. However, as an alternative approach, it may be reasonable to generate budget costs based on professional experience, either as a supplement to or instead of these. Such budget costs should be generated in the same manner as for any other cost plan that is prepared. The work content should be broken down into its discrete elements, so that each item of work can be measured into a quantity. It is then necessary to identify what monetary sum ('rate') is applied to these quantities, by using professional experience to compare past rates from similar projects or in published information. The rate that most accurately reflects both the work content and the nature of the project should be applied to the quantities and the budget cost generated.

Allowances for the cost of any access equipment such as scaffolding should be made, together with contractors' preliminaries/overheads. These should either be based on a percentage uplift, calculated upon experience as before, or by building them up, as a contractor would, from the individual elements. It is not acceptable to include provisional items or contingency sums. This is because it is not possible to claim a loss unless there is a quantifiable breach. While it is not unreasonable to include a contingency allowance in any normal budget, such an allowance does not relate to any quantified item and therefore cannot constitute a breach. If the works are already completed, any uncertain items will, as a consequence, have been quantified.

A similar approach and extent of effort should be applied to the remaining elements of the claim that are identified below. A lack of effort in finding out whether, for example, a building is elected for VAT or what the void rates are, is not acceptable and will lead to unnecessary disputes.

Consequential losses

In some circumstances a landlord will also suffer consequential losses as a result of the tenant's breaches. The most frequently claimed items flow from the amount of time that it takes to carry out the remedial works, but other heads of loss could be claimed, instead of or in addition to these. Such losses can include the need for temporary accommodation while the works are completed, interest charges if the works have to be funded, further damage caused to adjacent property (for example, if a leak passes into an adjacent flat), or, if the tenant is making the claim, loss of profit.

Drummond v S & U Stores Ltd (1981)

The landlord claimed, as one of its heads of claim, the loss of rent suffered by virtue of not being able to let the property during the period required to carry out the work of repair necessitated by the tenant's breach of covenant. It is often a significant item.

Other regular items of consequential loss include the service charge that the landlord can no longer recover and the void rates that the landlord is forced to pay during this period. The landlord is entitled to claim the void rates from the start of the period and to ignore the rates 'holiday' that accrues from the date that the property becomes vacant. This is because, had the tenant complied with its obligations, the landlord would have had the benefit of this period to cover the likely marketing void. It should be noted, however, that void rates are nil on industrial properties and only one-half the normal rates on other types of property.

It is important to distinguish between the period of time that would have been required to let the property, which the landlord would have encountered anyway, and the time that specifically relates to correcting the tenant's breaches of covenant. The landlord may not have been aware that the tenant was not going to comply with the terms of the lease until immediately after the lease ended. As such, the landlord's loss will accrue for the time that it would legitimately take to prepare specifications for the work, obtain tenders, decide which tender to select and appoint the contractor. Thereafter, there will be a period while the contractor mobilises its resources, followed by the actual construction period. The time allowed for these individual elements, or indeed, whether allowances are required for them at all, will depend on the nature of the particular claim being considered, and must reflect a reasonable assessment (see *Drummond v S & U Stores Ltd*). It is not reasonable to charge for the period that it takes to negotiate a settlement with the tenants. The landlord is under an obligation to mitigate its losses as far as reasonable and it should assume that it will start the works within a reasonable time, irrespective of whether there has been a settlement.

For these heads of loss to be claimed, it is imperative that they relate directly to the fundamental breaches of the lease (see *Scottish Mutual Assurance Society Ltd v British Telecommunications plc*). If a landlord actually carried out the works but also completed additional works, such as upgrading the lighting, it is more difficult to prove this direct relationship, and a claim for the consequential losses may fail, even if the basic claim is successful.

Contrary to these points, some leases specifically state that a tenant, if found to have breached the dilapidations covenants, will also be obliged to provide for a period of rent. Since this is a specific covenant and can only be satisfied by being performed, it is arguable that neither a diminution in value argument or proof that the works did not give cause to a loss of time in re-letting will affect this.

If a tenant knows that it is not going to be able to meet its repairing obligations, it could contemplate notifying the landlord of its predicament, so that the landlord would be able to prepare itself to have the works carried out. This might serve to reduce the time taken up after the end of the lease in inspecting the property and preparing specifications. In certain situations, this ought to lead to a reduction in the landlord's claim for consequential losses, as it would be under a duty to mitigate its losses by using this time to prepare itself.

Drummond v S & U Stores Ltd (1981)

Indeed that sort of issue was precisely what was in the mind of the judge in this case:

> 'After all it has been absolutely apparent to this landlord for a very long time that this tenant was not going to carry out the repairs. It must have been apparent to the landlord that the tenant was not going to reoccupy. The tenant, as I see it, had no rights to a new lease under the *Landlord and Tenant Act* 1954 and none has been suggested. I can see no reason why the landlord, had she wished to do so, should not have negotiated with a new tenant before the expiry of the old lease, and thus been ready the moment the old lease expired either to get a new tenant to do the repairs or to do them herself if she had sufficient funds to enable her to do so. The fact that she did not is a matter for her and her advisers. I suspect that it was because of these negotiations with the bus company that were likely to produce a more attractive proposition than any other tenant was able to offer, but that is perhaps an irrelevance. That, however, is my reason for not giving more than compensation for one quarter's loss of rent.'

Professional fees

In most situations, the landlord will also incur consultants' fees for the task of preparing a dilapidations schedule and a costed claim against the tenant. It is necessary to check the lease in each case – most modern leases specifically cover the recovery of fees in this situation. Such clauses deal with recovery in different ways and it may be possible that they can be recovered in some situations (such as when a section 146 notice is served), but not others. As noted above, even where there are clauses that allow a landlord to recover fees from a tenant, these must be reasonable in the light of the work done.

Maud v Sanders (1943)

If there is no specific clause within the lease, the courts generally will not allow a claim for the costs that arise as a result of the need to ascertain whether any breaches of the leases have occurred, rather than as a consequence of the breach itself.

In preparing the schedule of dilapidations, it may well be that additional specialist advice, from a mechanical and electrical services (M&E) engineer, or possibly a structural engineer, will be required. Indeed, as was highlighted in *Simmons v Dresden*, while the claim included M&E items, in the absence of any report or evidence from an M&E expert, the court had to regard those elements of the claim as being not proven.

Furthermore, it may be necessary formally to serve the schedule on the tenant, and if solicitors do this, a cost will be incurred. These additional items should be dealt with in the same manner as the main fee for preparing the schedule of dilapidations.

If the works are carried out by the tenant, it is probable that the landlord will arrange for a surveyor either to monitor the satisfactory completion of the tenants' works on site, or to negotiate a compensation payment in lieu of this. In such situations, it is less common for leases to have specific provisions relating to the recovery of these costs, and the correct approach to adopt in pre-litigation surveyor-to-surveyor negotiations is unclear.

In essence, if the matter were to go to trial, the court would have complete jurisdiction as to how the fees would be awarded. The general position is that 'costs follow the event' and the successful party to the litigation will have its costs paid by the unsuccessful party. However, the proportion of the costs paid will be assessed by the court in the light of the conduct of the parties and will be in proportion to the issues in dispute and the value of the claim. This means that if a landlord submits a dilapidations claim and is wholly successful, the tenant will pay both side's fees, but the costs the landlord will recover will only be in proportion to the issues of the case. That is, the fees must not be disproportionate to the amount of the actual claim made. In any event, there will rarely be a full reimbursement of costs, owing to the court's 'assessment' of fees, which always results in a proportion being irrecoverable. If the landlord's claim is unsuccessful, it will be obliged to pay not only its own advisers' fees but, in almost all cases, also those of the tenants (which will again be assessed in the light of the magnitude of the issues of the case, and so on).

A specific aim of the *Civil Procedure Rules* 1998 and the Protocol is to ensure that more disputes are resolved without litigation. The *Civil Procedure Rules* and Protocol do not provide any direction on how to deal with the costs of a pre-action negotiation, which is often a major area of contention. Therefore, a prudent tenant, in agreeing a settlement, may well need to make an offer in respect of the landlord's fees as well. If a landlord's claim is generally reasonably balanced, with the majority of the items validly included and costed, although there may be no obligation to do so, it could be appropriate to include at least some negotiation fees in a settlement offer. If the tenant were to take the converse view, it would run the risk that the matter would be taken to court and it would face higher costs. However, a landlord who submits an exaggerated or speculative claim should not expect to receive any negotiation fees in an offer, as it would be unlikely to get them if it went to court.

The situation in respect to fees for the negotiation of settlement is further complicated by Part 36 offers. These items were considered in Chapter 2, section 2.12.

Design, administration and other construction fees

In some instances a landlord will seek to execute the works itself. However, in most cases, it will employ advisers to arrange for this. In the latter case, the landlord will be entitled to claim the fees that it incurs in this. In circumstances where the landlord utilises other colleagues within its own organisation to execute the work, the situation is less clear. If there is a discrete internal charging mechanism for the use of the colleagues that can be clearly shown to exist, then this is probably a satisfactory measure of the damage incurred. It would also be possible to seek damages based on the loss of opportunity cost of a colleague who is purely salaried. This is more difficult to prove, however, as it is a liability that would have been incurred by the landlord anyway and should not, therefore, generally be used.

Typically, the landlord will require an architect or a surveyor to design, specify and administer the work. On occasions, specialist advice from either services consultants or a structural engineer will also be needed. Many situations will involve construction projects above the thresholds of the *Construction (Design and Management) Regulations* 1994, in which case the costs of a planning supervisor will also be a legitimate cost. There are circumstances where other specialists, such as a project manager or party wall expert, might be legitimately required, but these would be unusual.

Plough Investments Ltd v Manchester City Council (1989)

The fees included in a claim must be a fair representation of the likely cost to the landlord of the services to be rendered.

The test for the legitimacy of both the number of consultants required and the appropriate rates for their charges is what a reasonable landlord would do in this situation, if there was no possibility of seeking to recover the money by damages. The costs should therefore represent the likely market fees that would be incurred for each element being considered. The use of the old RICS scale of fees is not likely to be a fair measure of this, as it has now been withdrawn, but it would be rare that a fair fee would be above its levels (the RICS fee scale for building surveying was abolished in February 2000).

VAT

VAT will often be payable on the value of the construction work and the fees that form the basis of the dilapidations claim. In many situations, the landlord will not be able to recover the VAT that it incurs, and this will, therefore, represent a loss to the landlord, which can then be included as a head of claim. Where the failure to recover VAT stems from the breaches of the tenant's covenants, it will become a legitimate additional item to the claim.

It is appropriate that the landlord, or its consultants, should establish whether VAT is a valid head of loss before serving the claim on the tenant. Essentially, the landlord can only recover VAT in one of three situations, as described below.

1   Usually, the first matter to consider is the VAT status of the property (that is, whether it is elected for tax). Where the

landlord has elected to waive the exemption from VAT, or will have done by the time the work is to be executed, it can generally recover the VAT charged to it from HM Revenue & Customs. VAT will therefore not be a loss and cannot be included as a head of loss. A quick, but not conclusive, way to determine whether a property has been elected for tax is to review a previous rent demand. If it includes VAT on the rent, then it is likely that the property has been elected for tax.

2   For properties that are not elected for tax, it is necessary to consider whether the landlord is registered for VAT. Where it is, and is seeking to complete the works for its own occupation, then it will also be able to recover VAT on the works and associated fees. However, where a property is not elected for tax and works are being undertaken by the landlord in order to achieve a re-letting rather than for its own occupation, VAT cannot be recovered, irrespective of the VAT status of the landlord.

3   If the property is not elected for tax, and the landlord has agreed new terms for a re-letting to a third party, and that third party is registered for VAT, then any VAT on works to be executed as a term of that re-letting will be recoverable. At this point, even if the terms offered to the new tenant include elements of work above the usual market inducement owing to the presence of dilapidations items, VAT will not accrue on these (see *Drummond v S & U Stores Ltd* below).

In all remaining situations, a landlord will not be able to recover VAT, and it will become a valid addition to the landlord's claim.

Drummond v S & U Stores Ltd (1981)

When considering a claim that included a claim for VAT, the judge said:

'My mind has fluctuated about that question, but I have come to the conclusion in the end that the argument on behalf of the landlord is correct in relation to this matter. There are two reasons for that conclusion: the first is, as I suggested in argument, that if [the tenant's] argument is correct it means that, albeit the landlord may very well in fact re-let the premises, nevertheless the effect of depriving her of value added tax on the damages, or as part of the damages, would effectively be to close her other options, that is to say, if she changed her mind and decided that she would like to sell the premises and put the money to some other use but that she wanted to sell them in lease condition, then she would have to incur value added tax and she would not have recovered it as part of the damages ... I have come to the conclusion that the damages, if properly assessable on the basis of the cost of repair, should properly include also value added tax, or rather, should include an item equal to the amount of value added tax which the landlord would suffer on such costs.'

It is arguable, though, that it should not be paid in situations where the landlord does not actually intend to undertake the works.

Elite Investments Ltd v TI Bainbridge Silencers (No. 2) (1987)

The court was left with the impression that the landlords had no intention of doing any sort of work on the property. No evidence was put before it in relation to what the landlords might be wishing to do or considering doing. In those circumstances the case was readily distinguishable from the *Drummond* case. On that basis the court decided that the case was not one in which it could direct that assessed value added tax be added to the amount claimed.

However, since *Drummond v S & U Stores Ltd* it has become more difficult to adopt this position, and in any situation where there is a reasonable prospect that the landlord will complete the works at some time in the future, VAT will be a head of claim.

It should be noted that in some instances a dilapidations settlement could become combined with a surrender agreement that includes a surrender premium. In these instances, the application of VAT may not apply in the manner described above and separate tax advice will be required.

6.2.6.7 Betterment

In the event that the tenant does not do the work, the landlord will be faced with determining what works it wishes to complete to the property. Often, the landlord will wish to do works that are not exactly the same as the outgoing tenant's dilapidations liability; however, not all of the works that are outside the tenant's liability will bring about supercession. In many instances, especially if the additional items are small in number or consequence, the additional works will not conflict with or supersede the tenant's obligations. The landlord would therefore still be able to make a claim for the dilapidations items but must exclude the other items, which make up their 'betterment' works.

In such situations, it normally makes economic sense to complete these works as part of one overall project, as this can avoid the possibility of duplicated fees or preliminaries. In most cases it might seem that the fairest manner to approach the apportionment of these would be to pro rata them in proportion to the respective portions of betterment and the dilapidations items. In fact, they will either be fully included in the claim or superseded. However, if the extent of betterment is either particularly small or particularly substantial, this may not be the equitable course of action.

An example of where betterment may apply is where a tenant is required to completely rebuild a property if it has been destroyed. However, it will sometimes be the case that there is no alternative to the method or nature of the work required and if that results in the landlord being left with something new, then so be it. Another example of betterment in practice might be where an outgoing tenant is obliged to remove partitions from an internal office, decorate, repair the ceiling and renew carpets. If the landlord also wished to renew the lighting, in the process necessitating the renewal of the ceiling, this is likely to lead to supercession of the repairs to the ceiling but leave the remainder of the work within the tenant's liability. This is, however, a question of fact and degree, as it is possible to arrive at the point where there is so much betterment that the residual of dilapidations works become irrelevant. At this point, the loss in value that the remaining dilapidations items gives rise to becomes impossible to separate from the loss that flows from works that make up the whole project.

Stent v Monmouth DC (1987)

A defective wooden door could only sensibly be replaced with an aluminium door – clearly an improvement, but no allowance for betterment was made.

6.2.6.8 Assessing statutory damages

The amount of the diminution in a landlord's reversionary value is generally assessed by carrying out two valuations. The first assumes that the tenant's repairing obligations have been complied with and the second that the property is in its actual state of repair.

In carrying out these two valuations, it is important to fully consider the impact of the market on the value of the landlord's interest. This can best be done by considering who would be in the market for such an interest and the likely plans of such a purchaser in connection with the repair, refurbishment or re-letting of the property.

Having established the 'intention of the parties', it should be easier to establish the price that would be paid for the landlord's reversion at the valuation date on the 'before' and 'after' bases.

The landlord's reversion means the landlord's interest at the date of termination. This may be freehold or leasehold and one must value whatever is subsisting at the date of valuation. The date of valuation is the date of termination of the lease, when the tenant's covenant to yield up the property takes effect.

There are a number of issues to be considered when approaching a claim for damages where section 18(1) applies. These are looked at in greater detail below.

6.2.6.9 Diminution valuations

The landlord's actions

When considering a claim for damages where section 18(1) applies, one needs to consider exactly what the landlord's requirements are. It may want the property repaired or prefer a cash settlement.

It may intend to demolish or substantially refurbish a property, so as to render valueless the repair works required, or it may intend to sell the property for an alternative higher-value use.

It may well be that the landlord has made its intentions very clear. It may have served a section 25 notice under the *Landlord and Tenant Act* 1954, indicating that it would not be prepared to grant a new lease on one of the statutory grounds set out in section 30(1) of that Act. If one of the grounds cited is that which relates to an intended redevelopment or refurbishment of the property, it could significantly affect the landlord's claim for damages, in that the execution of such works is likely to bring into play the second limb of section 18(1). (By way of reminder, the second limb of section 18(1) can extinguish the rights of a landlord to claim damages for breach of the repairing covenant at the expiry of the term if it intends to demolish or substantially alter the property.)

However, such action on the part of the landlord does not necessarily imply that the tenant will be successful in arguing a 'nil' damages claim, as the landlord will have served its notice at least six months before expiry and circumstances may have changed. In order for the second limb of section 18(1) to take effect, there has to be a settled intention to demolish or carry out major works of refurbishment. It has generally been accepted that to prove a settled intention, one has to adduce similar evidence to that required when seeking possession under section 30 of the *Landlord and Tenant Act* 1954 for redevelopment. This includes providing evidence of board approval, planning permission, the availability of finance, and so on; the mere service of the section 25 notice will not in itself prove a settled intention and further proof will need to be provided if the court is to be persuaded.

The Protocol recommends that the landlord states its intentions. If it does not, the normally prudent surveyor representing a tenant should directly ask what the landlord's intentions are. The landlord is effectively obliged to answer such a request as, if it remains silent, it will have difficulty later proving any loss.

Items such as loss of rent and professional fees have been considered (briefly) in the context of a common law claim for damages (see 6.2.6.6, 'Heads of loss'). There is no reason why such items would not form part of the landlord's diminution valuation if they form part of the damage to the value of the reversion.

The tenant's position

The commentary in this section is divided under the following topics:

- general valuation points;
- alternative uses; and
- sale of property.

General valuation points

As mentioned above, the amount of the diminution in the value of the landlord's reversion is assessed by carrying out two valuations. The first is on the assumption that the tenant's repairing obligations have been complied with and the second on the basis that the property is in its actual state of disrepair. In carrying out these valuations, it is important to consider, among other things, the present and future state of the market; the extent to which the existence of disrepair will affect the landlord's ability to re-let the property or its rental value; and the likelihood or otherwise of the property being redeveloped or substantially altered, so as to extinguish the right to damages altogether. In other words, in the context of the market and the age of the property, it is essential to try to assess the landlord's likely intentions for the property.

If the tenant cannot prove that the landlord intends either to redevelop or substantially refurbish the property, it should look to see what works a hypothetical purchaser may need to carry out in order to re-let the property. If such a purchaser, in order to re-let the property, would be likely to carry out more substantial works than would be required to remedy the breach, then it will be necessary to consider which of the tenants' repairs would survive this upgrading. In such a case, the diminution in the landlord's reversion would be limited to the cost only of those repairs that would survive the refurbishment.

Alternative uses

The tenant should also consider alternative uses for the property. If a tenant can prove that an alternative use, for which planning permission would be granted, would produce a higher value than an existing use, it may be legitimate for this to form the basis of valuation. If this is the case, then any repair works that would be nullified by the change of use cannot be included in the claim for damages. For example, if an office property has a greater value if converted into flats, then any works of repair that would not be required for the conversion, such as repairs to a suspended ceiling, could not form part of the claim for damages. If the more valuable use resulted in demolition or substantial refurbishment of the property for an alternative use, then there could be no claim for damages at all.

Ultraworth Ltd v General Accident Fire & Life Assurance Corp plc (2000)

A detailed summary is appropriate. The question was whether the tenant was required to replace an ageing heating system in a five-storey office property that was let in 1973 on a 25-year full repairing and insuring lease. Following the expiry of the lease on 4 July 1998, the landlord sold the freehold in March 1999 to a developer (B Ltd) for £1m. B Ltd subsequently obtained planning permission to convert all of the properties, except the ground floor, into residential flats. During the discussions over the terminal schedule of dilapidations, the parties agreed that the building was not in the state of repair required by the covenant. However, the principal dispute was over the extent of the tenant's liability in connection with the poor state of the combined heating and air-conditioning system. The system was of a type that was no longer manufactured. The landlord maintained that the repairing covenant could only be performed by substantially replacing the entire system, at an estimated cost of £420,000. The tenant claimed that the system was capable of being repaired and argued for a figure not exceeding £100,000. However, the tenant further argued that as the property was subsequently disposed of for conversion into flats, the disrepair had not resulted in any diminution in the value of the landlord's reversion. The judge preferred both the technical and marketing evidence given by the tenant's experts and held that no loss had been sustained by the landlord. There were three points of particular interest in this decision:

(a)   It was confirmed that the works required to the heating and air-conditioning system were works of repair, as opposed to works of renewal. It is well established that repair can consist of renewal of parts and that the court should consider, among other things, the nature, extent and cost of the proposed remedial works, the value of the property and its expected life span. As always, it is a matter of degree. (See the case examples given in 2.1.)

(b)   The landlord failed to establish that the work proposed by the tenant would be insufficient. So long as the repaired system worked substantially as well as the original system, there was no requirement that it should require as little maintenance as a new system.

(c)   The court was satisfied on the evidence put before it that, even if the system had been repaired:

   (i)   the property would not have attracted a potential occupier or investor; and

   (ii)   B Ltd would not have paid a higher price, because its scheme required a different system altogether.

The fact that a landlord decides to retain a property for offices and therefore pursues a claim for damages, rather than choosing to convert the property into residential use, will not necessarily defeat a tenant's claim that there is no damage to the reversion. If the higher value can be proved to be in residential conversion or redevelopment, then the landlord's claim could fail.

Sale of property

Another common scenario is that a property is sold with an outstanding dilapidations claim. The position of the parties in relation to the breach of covenant remains, in theory, the same. However, in practice, the sale can have a significant effect on the assessment of damages, for the following reasons:

- The sale price achieved for the property in its existing state of disrepair fixes the 'before' valuation. This is an actual figure and therefore less open to dispute.

- The existence of an actual sale price also indicates that there is a ready market for the property in its unrepaired state, which could make it more difficult for the landlord to argue that the cost of works should represent the damages. However, if the purchaser carries out the repairs, then this is strong evidence, from the landlord's point of view, that the works were necessary, and it is reasonable to assume that it would have achieved a higher price for its interest had the tenant complied with its repairing obligations and yielded up the property in repair.

- It may in fact be difficult for the landlord to argue that it has suffered any loss at all. This will primarily depend, among other things, on the plans of the new owner for the property. If a purchaser buys an office block to convert it into flats, then one can assume that such a conversion will produce a higher value than the existing use. Therefore, there would be no damage to the reversion, as the landlord would have benefited from an enhanced price. It is also probable that the conversion works would nullify a large element of the works of repair.

- If an investment property is sold to a purchaser for its own occupation, the matter is further complicated, as an enhanced price may have been paid to reflect the benefits of owner occupation. In these circumstances, the state of repair may not have had a detrimental effect on value. It is, after all, not unknown for an unmodernised house to sell at a very similar price to its updated equivalent, because of the desire of owner-occupiers to 'stamp their identity' on the property.

6.2.6.10 Factors influencing the valuation

Factors considered in this section include the following:

- deterioration of the property after expiry;
- reinstatement;
- the effect of extreme market conditions;
- assumption that a transaction will take place;
- the existence of subtenants;
- negative values;
- lack of evidence;
- subsequent events;
- refurbishment and redevelopment.

Deterioration of the property after expiry

If a property deteriorates after a landlord resumes possession, the tenant will not be liable to compensate the landlord for that deterioration. The tenant's liability could be considerably diminished if there is a lack of evidence regarding the condition of the property at the expiry of the lease. The existence of a schedule of condition together with a photographic record of the state of the property at expiry will therefore be very useful evidence of the state of repair.

Reinstatement

Reinstatement under licence is a separate covenant to the repairing covenant and is outside the scope of section 18(1) of the 1927 Act. Such items of work could in theory be contained in a separate schedule and form part of an additional claim for damages, which may not necessarily be subject to the diminution argument. The same argument applies to redecoration works. In practice, however, these items usually appear in the schedules prepared by building surveyors, and as long as the references to their origin are stated within the schedule, it is likely that the court will accept that reinstatement and redecoration have been requested (confirmed in *Westminster City Council v HSBC Bank plc*, see 2.5).

The effect of extreme market conditions

In looking at the 'before' and 'after' valuations in a poor market, the argument that the property would not let whatever condition it was in is quite persuasive. For example, it may be argued that the market value of a property is simply unaffected by the state of repair, as it would be unlettable and therefore have no value even if it was in good repair. This argument is particularly relevant to properties constructed in the late 1960s and early 1970s. The future of such properties is either demolition, substantial refurbishment or constructive vandalism (to save through empty rates). Dilapidations cannot be an issue in these cases. Paradoxically, the same argument may be run on very different grounds in a strong market, where a property could be regarded as ripe for redevelopment so that the state of the property is of no consequence.

Assumption that a transaction will take place

An argument for 'nil' damages, unless as a result of the implementation of the second limb of section 18(1) of the 1927 Act, is unlikely to find favour with the court, which is not well disposed to extreme arguments. Although a property may be unsaleable or unlettable, the court, when assessing damages, will assume that the property has a value. In other words, as in many cases of contractual and statutory valuations, it has to be assumed that a transaction will take place. There is no specific reference in section 18(1) to a willing purchaser and a willing vendor, or even a willing lessor and a willing lessee, and the value of the property in repair and disrepair must therefore be assessed on the assumption that there are hypothetical parties. The valuation exercise is artificial, but this artificiality should not be carried further than is necessary by assuming that the parties are desperate or unaware of their negotiating positions.

The existence of subtenants

The presence of subtenants in the property who are likely to renew their leases on full repairing and insuring terms would support an argument that there is no diminution in value and therefore no grounds for a claim for damages. This would be true unless the disrepair was so severe that it would affect the value of the landlord's reversion.

Negative values

Shortlands Investments Ltd v Cargill plc (1995)

A landlord can be compensated for 'an even greater negative value'. The argument that a negative or very low value of a property in repair means no damage to the reversion was dismissed in this case, where it was accepted that, out of repair, the value could in fact be a greater negative, for which the landlord should be compensated. Thus, it was accepted that holding property, unlike chattels, could have a cost implication, such as outgoing liabilities, whether it was income-producing or not.

Some circumstances likely to give rise to negative values are large fixed outgoings, such as head rents or rates and service charges that the landlord has to pay irrespective of whether the property is income-producing. In addition, when long void periods are anticipated, receipt of income is significantly deferred, thus reducing capital value substantially.

If a property is listed, there may be no opportunity for the landlord to pursue other avenues such as demolition or even substantial refurbishment. There are, therefore, very few options open to the landlord and, in these circumstances, the property could well have a negative value. In these instances, it is also likely that the cost of repairs will be the measure of damages, as the property will have to be repaired to comply with the obligations of planning legislation relating to listings.

It is interesting to note that the method adopted in *Shortlands v Cargill* is the only method of valuing a diminution that has actually been set out in a published court decision. As such, some argue that this is the appropriate method for assessing all diminution in value. It might also be noted at this point that it will not always be necessary for a valuer to carry out a valuation to assess loss – a building surveyor needs to and can often give a realistic assessment, removing from consideration those items which would be superseded by the landlord's works.

Lack of evidence

If market conditions have resulted in an absence of direct evidence as to values of similar properties in and out of repair, this will result in the cost of the work being of greater significance in calculating the damage to the reversion. The courts seem to be attracted to the cost of works as the measure of damages, owing to its simplicity and realism. A lack of market evidence will further support this view.

Subsequent events

In markets where there is little transactional evidence, the relevance of events occurring after the term date may also be more significant. While such events do not extinguish damages, they are strong evidence of future intentions. As long as they are not too remote from the valuation date, they could provide an insight into the way in which the hypothetical purchaser might have looked at the reversion on the termination date. This may involve demolition or perhaps a sale to a purchaser who substantially refurbishes the property.

It may be that the landlord re-lets the property after the termination date on the basis that the incoming tenant carries out works of repair in exchange for a rent-free period or capital contribution towards the works, as occurred in *Shortlands v Cargill*. This is all evidence of the market approach and, if the notional purchaser can be shown to be likely to have acted in a similar manner, then the diminution will be the value of the lost rent or the capital contribution.

If, without doing the repairs, the landlord sells the property, then the terms of the sale are a good indication of the value in the actual condition.

However, it is important to remember that the valuer cannot have regard to matters that he or she could not have foreseen at the date of valuation.

Refurbishment and redevelopment

When market conditions are buoyant, dilapidations claims can be defeated if the landlord intends to redevelop or refurbish. This is unlikely to be an option in a poor market and in these circumstances landlords will be able to make and sustain a dilapidations claim. However, if a tenant can prove that refurbishment is a viable option that produces more value for the landlord than just repairing the property, the argument may find favour with the court. In such a situation, a dilapidations claim could be significantly reduced, as the refurbishment would be likely to nullify at least some of the repair works. Conversely, as any refurbishment undertaken in a poor market is likely to be only marginally profitable, a successful dilapidations claim will be seen by many landlords as a contribution towards the project costs.

If the landlord intends substantially to refurbish the property, there is every possibility that the claim for damages will be significantly reduced, if not entirely extinguished. Therefore, if a landlord is keen to maintain a claim for damages, it needs to consider carefully its decisions about the future of the property. The landlord must be conscious about the effect of steps such as working up its refurbishment scheme, obtaining planning permission, and having contractors waiting to move on site, as this state of readiness could count against it, by indicating that it is going to carry out substantial work that would nullify or diminish a claim for damages by virtue of the second limb of section 18(1) of the 1927 Act.

If the landlord does not have plans for the refurbishment of the property, it may well be able to negotiate a settlement for damages against a costed schedule of dilapidations. It can then put this towards a refurbishment scheme, should it subsequently choose to carry one out. However, if it were minded to do so, the tenant could use the fact of refurbishment as evidence to support a contention that such work was the landlord's true intention all along. Alternatively, if the landlord proposes only to refurbish the interior of the property, then it is entitled to serve a schedule in respect of the exterior and structural works (and possibly the plant and machinery), as these elements would be unaffected by the proposal. An alternative, but similar, situation would involve the cost of stripping out internal partitions and fixtures and fittings. If these would have to be removed as part of the repair work, then this would be a legitimate claim.

6.2.6.11 Non-section 18(1) losses

There are some breaches of covenant to which section 18(1) does not apply, e.g. a breach of the covenant to decorate. In such cases, the approach to quantifying the damages payable to the landlord will depend on the precise circumstances of each case. In some instances, the damages will equate to the cost of putting the breach right, together with an allowance for the time it will take to do so. In other cases, the damage to the reversion will be the appropriate measure.

In practice, the main consideration when deciding if the claim should be based on the cost of the necessary work or the damage to the reversion is whether it is reasonable in all the circumstances for the landlord to carry out the work. In some cases, the cost of the work would be wholly disproportionate to the benefit that would be achieved and in those conditions, the damage to the reversion would be more likely to be the appropriate measure.

Ruxley Electronics & Construction Ltd v Forsyth (1996)

The claimant had built a swimming pool that was about nine inches shallower than specified. The pool was still safe to dive into, but the defendant wanted the claimant to rebuild the pool. The cost of doing so would have been in the region of £21,500. The court held that to require rebuilding was unreasonable and out of all proportion to the benefit that would be obtained – the loss would be assessed on the basis of difference in value.

Another distinction with regard to a claim to which section 18(1) applies is the date of valuation of the claim. Where section 18(1) applies, the valuation date is the end of the term. Where it does not apply, it is more likely to be the date of the breach, although that is not a hard and fast rule. There will be circumstances where a later date is appropriate. Of particular relevance when considering this issue is the date when the work can actually be carried out. It may be that for some legitimate reason the work cannot be carried out until some time after the breach – if, for example, that is when the landlord can first gain access to carry it out.

If the appropriate measure of damages is the diminution to the reversion, then the principles applied where section 18(1) applies will be relevant.

6.2.6.12 Damages for failure to reinstate or to decorate

There are often obligations to reinstate alterations carried out during the term, with such obligations either in the lease or, more frequently, in a licence for alterations.

As this is not a covenant to repair, section 18(1) does not apply. Although the common law measure of damages will therefore be the correct approach, there is no obvious distinction between a covenant to reinstate and other covenants to which section 18(1) does not apply. Consequently, the points made in section 6.2.6.11 apply equally here. In other words, damages could be assessed by reference to the cost of carrying out the work the tenant should have done, if it would be reasonable to do that work, or by reference to the damage to the reversion. It is more likely to be the former if, as in a case where section 18(1) applies, the landlord has actually carried out the work or satisfies the court that it intends to.

6.2.7 Damages: tenant's claim against the landlord

Unlike a landlord's claim for damages against a tenant, there are no statutory restrictions on a tenant's claim for damages against a landlord.

Consequently, the measure of the tenant's damages is derived from common law. Probably the two most significant cases are as follows.

Calabar Properties Ltd v Stitcher (1983) and Wallace v Manchester City Council (1998)

In summary, the approach is to identify what sum will put the tenant back into the position it would have been but for the breach of covenant by the landlord. Linked with that is a comparison of the property as it was during the period of the landlord's breach with what it should have been had there been no breach. If the tenant remained in occupation during the period of the breach, then it will be entitled to be compensated for the loss of comfort and convenience it suffered from occupying a property that was out of repair. If the tenant was forced to sell or sublet the property as a result of the landlord's disrepair, then it will be entitled to be compensated by reference to the consequential reduction in the price or rent received. The claim will run from the moment the landlord was in breach of covenant (*Wallace* concerned residential property).

To maximise its chances of making a successful claim for damages against the landlord, the tenant should make the landlord aware of the problem as soon as possible and give it every opportunity to take remedial action, including allowing the landlord access to the property demised to carry out the work. The tenant should also ensure that the landlord is aware of the potential categories of loss it might suffer if it does not act – for example, that the tenant may not be able to sell at the price it would otherwise have achieved or might not be able to use the whole or part of the property for its normal and permitted purpose.

Given the distinctions that apply where the tenant stays in occupation and where it leaves, the two areas will be considered separately below.

6.2.7.1 The tenant remains in occupation

On the face of it, the measure of damages in this instance is assessed by valuing the property in its condition where the landlord is in breach and comparing this with the value the property would have had to the tenant had the covenant been satisfied. In a similar way to assessing the damage to the reversion where the landlord claims damages against a tenant, the cost to the tenant of remedying the landlord's breach may be an indicator of the damages due to the tenant, plus an amount for inconvenience and discomfort.

One way of approaching such damages is to assess a notional reduction in the rent. Another is to allow a global amount for discomfort and inconvenience. For example, where part of a property cannot be used, the court may attribute a part of the rent to it and multiply that by the period of time it is out of use. The court will, however, be concerned to adopt such an approach on the basis of the true rental value of the property, rather than the actual rent payable.

Credit Suisse v Beegas Nominees Ltd (1994)

Although the case of *Wallace v Manchester City Council* concerned residential property, the concept of damages for inconvenience has been applied to commercial property and an amount allowed for inconvenience to a corporate tenant's staff and customers, where £40,000 was awarded.

Further, if the tenant's belongings have been damaged as a result of the landlord's breach, then a claim might be made for the consequential loss. If the landlord's breach has resulted in damage to the part of the property demised to the tenant, then the cost of putting that right might also be claimed. For example, the roof might leak and the water penetration then damages the internal decorations.

If the tenant has been forced to carry out the work itself, then the resultant cost could be the subject of a claim (see 6.2.8, 'Tenant to carry out work'). However, credit might have to be given for that part of the cost that the tenant would have had to pay to the landlord if it had properly carried out the work when due.

6.2.7.2 The tenant leaves and returns or sells or sublets

If the damage consequent on the landlord's breach is such that the tenant has to leave the property, occupy (and pay for) alternative accommodation, and then return to deal with any redecoration or similar activity, then all the resultant costs (provided they are reasonably incurred and reasonable as to amount) can form part of its claim for damages against the landlord.

If the tenant has lost profits as a result of the landlord's breach, there may be a claim, but it depends on whether such losses could be said to have been contemplated by the parties.

If the tenant sells its leasehold interest before the work is carried out, and if there is a difference in the price that would have been achieved if the landlord had complied with its covenant, then that difference will be a measure of the tenant's damages.

If the tenant had wanted to sell, but could not, as a result of the landlord's breaches, then the tenant may be able to claim any loss of premium and any costs associated with retaining the property (including outgoings, rent and service charges – see *Credit Suisse v Beegas Nominees Ltd*).

If the tenant had wanted to sublet and could not, or was only able to do so at a reduced rent, there may be a further claim. However, there may also be an argument by the landlord that such a claim is too remote and that it cannot be held responsible for such loss. As is so often the case, the outcome will depend on the particular circumstances.

6.2.8 Tenant to carry out work

If the landlord has failed to carry out work to an area of a property that is demised to the tenant, then it seems clear that the tenant can carry out the work in default.

If the landlord has failed to carry out work to an area of the property that is not demised to the tenant, then it also seems clear that the tenant has an implied right (there may be an express term, too) to enter that part of the property, particularly if the tenant is suffering damage as a result of the landlord's breach, and carry out the work.

In either case, if the tenant is planning to seek to recover the cost from the landlord, it would be best advised to notify the landlord first that it considers the landlord to be in breach of its obligations and invite the landlord to carry out the work, or at the very least, inspect the area concerned. If the landlord does not carry out the work or inspect, the tenant should make sure to retain evidence (preferably including photographs) of the breach by the landlord, so that the tenant can answer any later assertion by the landlord that it was not in breach or that the work carried out by the tenant was unnecessary or unreasonable as to extent or cost.

6.2.9 Tenant's set-off (or withholding sums due to the landlord)

If a tenant has a damages claim against a landlord, then although it can make a claim against the landlord or a counterclaim to a claim brought against it by the landlord in court proceedings, it can also seek to 'recover' its damages by setting them off against monies due to the landlord. Where such a remedy is possible, it is very convenient, because it avoids the usual problems associated with making a positive claim, particularly with regard to costs and delay.

Connaught Restaurants v Indoor Leisure (1994)

However, in some leases there is a covenant by the tenant to pay monies to the landlord without set-off. If such words exist, then the tenant cannot avail itself of this remedy. Any lesser words – for example, to pay without deduction – are not sufficient to exclude the tenant's right to set-off.

Where the right to set-off is available, then although it is easier to exercise if the tenant has carried out the work in default of the landlord having done so (see 6.2.8, 'Tenant to carry out work'), it is not imperative; the tenant can exercise a right of set-off in respect of its as yet unquantified losses.

Bearing in mind that the landlord may disagree with the tenant's action, the prudent tenant will notify the landlord of the problems that have resulted in the tenant suffering loss, give the landlord an opportunity to take remedial action and notify it that, in default, the tenant will exercise its right of set-off. The tenant should also be careful not to exaggerate its claim, as the landlord may demonstrate that there is still a net payment (of, say, rent) due to it and take enforcement action.

6.2.10 Insolvency

The impact of the *Insolvency Acts* and related Acts on making claims has already been mentioned in 6.2.1, 'Forfeiture'.

Taking action under the *Insolvency Acts* may in itself be an appropriate method of enforcing the terms of the tenancy. It is not within the remit of this book to consider insolvency proceedings in any depth. If it appears that such action is warranted, specialist legal advice should be sought.

However, some key points to note are as follows:

- There must be a clear debt owed by the landlord or tenant in excess of £750.

- The debt should be undisputed. If it is disputed, then insolvency action – whether by winding up a company (putting it into liquidation) or making an individual bankrupt – will not be appropriate and the proceedings will probably not be allowed to continue.

- There must be a quantifiable debt. As a result, insolvency action is most likely to be relevant in the context of a dilapidations claim where a *Jervis v Harris* clause (after *Jervis v Harris*) has been operated and the landlord's costs quantified, or where a claim for damages has been made and is to be enforced.

A liquidator or trustee in bankruptcy has the right to disclaim onerous property. This could result in the lease coming to an end and the landlord finding itself in possession, with not only a rent void but also an obligation to pay the rates.

Putting a landlord or tenant into liquidation or making it bankrupt may have the result that, owing to the restrictions contained in the *Insolvency Acts*, the tenant or landlord finds that by its own actions it cannot enforce the terms of the tenancy.

6.2.11 Repudiation and quitting the property

In contract law, where a party to a contract is in serious breach, it is generally open to the other party to accept that breach as repudiating the contract – that is, bringing it to an end.

There has been significant debate as to whether the principle applies to leases. Although the debate has not finally been resolved, it seems that the current prevailing view is that it does.

If so, then where a landlord is so seriously in breach of its obligations concerning the condition of the property occupied by the tenant that the tenant simply cannot derive any benefit from the property, it appears that the tenant can contend that the landlord's breach is a repudiatory breach and that the lease is at an end, handing back the keys as evidence of its acceptance of the repudiatory breach. If the right exists, then the tenant must not delay in exercising it, as such delay may result in the right being lost.

As the law in this area is not clear and beyond doubt, the tenant should be advised to seek urgent specialist legal advice on the issue before it loses the right, should the right exist as a matter of law.

6.2.12 Frustration

As in the case of repudiation, frustration is a concept that applies to contracts.

National Carriers Ltd v Panalpina (Northern) Ltd (1981)

It has been held that the principle of frustration applies to leases.

In brief, frustration arises in instances where, when neither party to the contract or, in this case, the lease, is at fault, an event occurs that the contract had not provided for that so changes the position of the parties and the contract that the contract is to be regarded as being at an end. The lease might be frustrated, for example, where there is some catastrophic event that destroys the property. Otherwise, it is difficult to envisage other circumstances where the principle might apply in the context of the condition of the property.

If there is a dramatic, unenvisaged change to the property, and it is thought that the contract or lease has been frustrated, specialist legal advice should be sought.

Index

The *Case in Point* series

The *Case in Point* series is an exciting new set of concise practical guides to legal issues in land, property and construction. Written for the property professional, they get straight to the key issues in a refreshingly jargon-free style.

Areas covered:

Negligence in Valuation and Surveys
Stock code: 6388
Published: December 2002

Party Walls
Stock code: 7269
Published: May 2004

Service Charges
Stock code: 7272
Published: June 2004

Estate Agency
Stock code: 7472
Published: July 2004

Rent Review
Stock code: 8531
Published: May 2005

Expert Witness
Stock code: 8842
Published: August 2005

Lease Renewal
Stock code: 8711
Published: August 2005

VAT in Property and Construction
Stock code: 8840
Published September 2005

Construction Adjudication
Stock code: 9040
Published October 2005

If you would like to be kept informed when new *Case in Point* titles are published, please e-mail **rbmarketing@rics.org.uk**

All RICS Books titles can be ordered direct by:

☎   Telephoning 0870 333 1600 (Option 3)

🖱   Online at www.ricsbooks.com

📠   E-mail mailorder@rics.org.uk

15 A False
   B True
   C True
   D False
   E True

The choroid which runs from the posterior pole to the ora serrata is thicker posteriorly (0.22 mm) than anteriorly (0.1 mm). The ciliary vessels and nerves run in the lamina fusca of the sclera and the perichoroidal space to reach the anterior portion of the globe. Since retinal capillaries are absent at the fovea (foveal avascular zone), the choriocapillaris – the sole vascular supply to this area – is densest here. The choriocapillaris supplies the outer third of the retina up to and including the outer plexiform layer.

16 A False
   B False
   C False
   D False
   E False

The retina contains ≈ 20 times as many cones (≈ 6.5 million) as rods (≈ 120 million). It extends ≈ 1 mm further anteriorly on the medial side of the globe than the lateral, with the insertions of medial and lateral rectus being good approximations to the positions of the underlying ora serrata. The 5 million retinal pigment epithelial cells have a heavily folded outer surface lying against Bruch's membrane, and their inner surface possesses microvilli that interdigitate with the photoreceptors' outer segments. The rods are 100–120 μm long, whereas the cones are about 70 μm in length. The cell bodies of ganglion cells vary greatly in size due to the presence of midget ganglion cells.